Tears at
Bedtime

To Heather and Sarah, who have stood by me
through bad times and good times.

Tears at Bedtime

Tom Wilson
with Andrew Crofts

arrow books

Published by Arrow Books 2007

6 8 10 9 7

This book is a work of non-fiction based on the life, experiences and recollections of the author. In some limited cases names of people, places, dates, sequences or the detail of events have been changed to protect the privacy of others. The author has stated to the publishers that, except in such minor respects not affecting the substantial accuracy of the work, the contents of this book are true.

First published in Great Britain in 2007 by Arrow Books
The Random House Group Limited
20 Vauxhall Bridge Road, London, SW1V 2SA

www.rbooks.co.uk

Addresses for companies within The Random House Group Limited can be found at: www.rbooks.co.uk/environment

The Random House Group Limited Reg. No. 954009

A CIP catalogue record for this book
is available from the British Library

ISBN 9780099517726

The Random House Group Limited supports The Forest Stewardship Council (FSC), the leading international forest certification organisation. All our titles that are printed on Greenpeace approved FSC certified paper carry the FSC logo. Our paper procurement policy can be found at: www.rbooks.co.uk/environment

Typeset by SX Composing DTP, Rayleigh, Essex
Printed in the UK by CPI Bookmarque, Croydon, CR0 4TD

Introduction

There are many dedicated people working with children from families who can't cope, doing brilliant jobs: social workers, care workers and other professional staff who help to raise healthy, happy children in difficult circumstances. David Murphy was very nearly one of them.

As the housefather of the children's home we were taken to when it was decided that our mum and dad were unfit parents, David Murphy was being given a chance to change and shape our young lives for the better, along with many others. Most of what he did for us during the daylight hours was exactly what was required of him, but under the cover of night, or in secret moments during the day, something evil took hold of him and destroyed all the good he was achieving. It wasn't just me who was being hurt, although I had no way of knowing that at the time because when you are a small child you feel the whole world revolves around you and what happens to you. It doesn't matter what is going on even two streets away; if you are feeling frightened and insecure in your own world that is all you care about, because you have no experience of anything else and no way of reaching out past the bad stuff.

When someone starts their life at the bottom of the social pile, rejected and defenceless, you would hope that the only way for them to go is up. But for me this did not happen. What started badly grew a great deal more brutal and miserable, and it would be nearly fifty years before I would finally be able to find some peace.

In no way do I want to undermine the good work of the many because of the wickedness of a few, but if reading this book makes just one adult realise that with some simple acts of kindness he or she can change a child's life for ever, then it has been worth writing.

Chapter One

I'm lying in the dark, very small and very frightened.
I can hear the peaceful breathing of the other boys in
the beds around me, all of them safely asleep. I strain
my ears for any sound that will tell me whether he's
approaching through the dark house, but it's always
impossible to hear him until it's too late and he's right
there beside me. I can never tell whether this will be
one of the nights when he will come for me. I won't
know until I sense him leaning over the bed, pulling
back the covers, lifting me up out of the warmth and
carrying me off to his own cold sheets.

Such nightmares still haunt me even now that I'm
a grown man, and take time to dispel even once my

eyes are open. When Heather and I wake up together in the caravan in the early morning we are a million miles away from those dark, sinister dormitories. We can hear the chatter of the monkeys, the roaring of the lions and the screams of the peacocks drifting across from the other side of the park. We are living in Flamingo Land, in Yorkshire, a place where we always used to bring the children for their holidays and which we never wanted to leave. It is where we so often dreamed of one day staying permanently, believing even as we dreamed that it could never be more than a fantasy, an escape from the real world. But dreams, surprisingly, can sometimes come true.

Flamingo Land is a long way from the council estates of Kirkcaldy, in Scotland, where my family lived when I was young and where many of them still battle on, trying to stay out of debt and out of prison at the same time as bringing up their children and struggling to keep them away from drugs and the crime that inevitably follows them. It's a dangerous world for young people out there on the big estates, but not here, not while they are in Flamingo Land. Here they are guarded and watched over, disciplined and entertained. They don't mind being told they can't spit or fight one another, if it means they can ride the big dipper and plunge down the water flume.

When the gates to Flamingo Land are opened for a new day a stream of cars and coaches begins to pour through into the acres of car parks that have been silent and deserted all night. Families who have probably been on the road for hours emerge, hungry and excited. The peaceful dawn sounds from the zoo are replaced with the noise of happy crowds disappearing through the turnstiles and the hum of machinery as the giant rides fire up into life.

For the rest of the day the backing track to our peaceful new lives is the joyful screams of holiday-makers being hurtled around the big rides that rise up, then swoop and plunge down outside the French windows of the caravan. There is music and laughter and shouting and all seems well with the world.

This is a place where children of all ages come to escape the pressures and worries of their everyday lives, to frighten themselves on purpose or just to hang out with friends. It's a place where it is possible to believe that life could always be good and that childhood can be a magical time. Adults come partly because the children make them, and maybe partly to recapture something carefree from their own pasts; or perhaps to search for some kind of happiness they never experienced when they were young and feel they are entitled to at least taste for a day.

Flamingo Land is like the childhood I never had, my own private Never-Never Land. Watching the groups of young people coming and going, I wonder sometimes what is going on in their heads. Do they carry terrible, dark secrets like I once did? Have they had experiences that they can't even bring themselves to think about, let alone tell anyone else about? I guess we'll never know what proportion of people suffer abuse as children because so many of us don't talk about it, choose to forget it or at least push the memories out of sight. Some people say it is far more widespread than anyone imagines, while others say that such claims are wildly exaggerated. It has even been suggested that most people who claim to have been abused are making it up, or imagining things that never actually happened. At least now I can point to the evidence of my own past, and that of the others who were suffering in silence alongside me, and know that I didn't imagine it. It really did happen.

Heather and I have been coming to Flamingo Land for seventeen years as visitors, but we have only been able to make our dream of moving here come true because the authorities have finally accepted responsibility for what happened to me all those years ago. Nearly fifty years after it all started someone has at last believed what I've told them, apologised and tried to make it up to me. But there's a lot to make up, years that are impossible to replace, pain that can never be erased. I was just a baby when the council took responsibility for me and allowed one man to destroy my life.

Chapter Two

Those of you who have small babies, imagine for a moment having them taken away from you and put into a care home to be brought up by people you know nothing about. Walk down any street and look at all the strangers around you; are there any you would be happy just to hand your baby over to, trusting them to do the right thing? But that, more or less, is how my journey began.

At just ten months old I was much too young to know anything about what happened the first time I was taken away from my parents by Fife Council and placed in the care of Greenbanks Children's Home in Leven. None of us can ever really know what was done to us when we were babies, although family and friends can sometimes help fill in the blanks with their memories. A mother might tell a story down the years about how a butterfingered father dropped his baby the first time he held it. What must have been a trauma at the time becomes a funny family anecdote, so the child it happened to knows that it is true even if he or she can't remember the actual incident, but I have no witnesses to step forward and speak of what my life must have been like at that time.

I may have no memory of what happened to me in those few years I spent in Greenbanks, and no witnesses to fill in the gaps, but I do know from the records that the home was closed down during the 1960s amidst accusations of child abuse. I also know that the building was razed to the ground, as if such an act would cleanse the site of the sins it played host to, so I can't even go back to visit it to see if some detail of the building might jog my memory or resurrect any ghosts from the past. I later met another boy who was in Greenbanks at the same time as me and he could remember being abused when he was six or seven years old, but nothing he described brought back any memories for me.

To the authorities at the time I would imagine I was more of an inconvenient statistic than a person; one more problem baby amongst hundreds of others, coming from a troublesome family that shouldn't really have been allowed to have children at all. But you can't stop people from having babies just because they're too poor to feed and clothe them properly, or too ignorant to know the right way to bring them up. Once the babies are with us we have to work out the best way to help them survive and thrive, because at that stage nothing is their fault, they are still entirely blameless. They are innocent.

Nothing ever stopped Mum from having babies. I dare say we were all conceived when she'd had a few drinks and caution held no appeal. Neither she nor Dad ever had any regular work, so over the years she produced ten children with no way of supporting them other than by going to the Welfare with her hand out. Dad was always in the pub, probably to avoid her angry ways and the reality of what had become a very downtrodden life for him. Whatever it was they were doing, however they were living, the social services obviously decided very early on that Mum and Dad were not capable of looking after my brother Jocky and me, their two first-born children.

Jocky was with me right from the start in Greenbanks, but he's only about three years older than me, so he wouldn't be able to remember that time either. Even if he was the sort of man who talked about emotional things, he wouldn't be able to tell me anything about what might have gone on back then. He was little more than a baby himself.

I was known by everyone as Tommy in those days. Since then people have called me Tom, or Tam if they are Scottish, or even Thomas sometimes if they are being formal. Tommy now seems like someone else to me, and what happened to him seems like it took place in another world or in a bad dream. But he wasn't someone else, and the things that happened to Tommy were very real and turned him into the man I am today.

Over the years I have heard rumours about what might have happened to the children in Greenbanks during the time Jocky and I were there, but I have no way of knowing if they are true or not, or whether any of the things that people talk about happened to either of us. I'm sure I never will find out anything now and I'm resigned to that. I have more than enough later memories to fuel my nightmares.

When I was four and Jocky was almost seven, we were both transferred from Greenbanks to another children's home called St Margaret's in Elie, a big Victorian house standing on the beach staring out at the forbidding, slate-grey North Sea, which was usually being whipped up by violent storms, lashing us with salty spray every time we stepped outside. The home was run by a couple called the Gibsons when we got there and that is almost all I can remember of it at that stage. On and off it was going to be my home and prison, my playground and my torture chamber for the next eight years of my life.

I may not know what went on in my early years in the secrecy of those children's homes, but I do know that by the time I was five they had decided to send me to Ovenstone, a children's psychiatric hospital, so something must already have been going badly wrong. No one sends a child to a psychiatric ward for no reason, not even a social worker.

There were times during those eight years when the social services sent us back home for trial periods, to see if Mum and Dad had mended their ways and actually could look after us; so I did have some idea what life would have been like had we been allowed to stay with them full-time. Every day that I was in St Margaret's I was longing to be back home with Mum regardless of her faults, but going on the evidence they had at the time, the authorities probably made the right decision in taking us away, they just chose the wrong person to give us to.

Not long after arriving at St Margaret's Jocky and I were taken back home for our first trial period with Mum and Dad. I was thrilled to think that my parents actually wanted me back, but it can't have gone well because the social workers came for us again within a few months. My memory of the event is hazy, but I do remember fighting the social worker who was trying to force me into the car, bracing my legs against the side like a toddler resisting his pushchair, shouting that I didn't want to go with them. In the end I was more or less picked up and thrown onto the back seat, kicking and screaming and quite possibly biting. They had decided to take us back to St Margaret's.

Because of what was to happen over the years to come in St Margaret's, I recently returned to Fife to research the local social services records. As I pored over the dusty papers, thirsty for any information about my younger self that I could find, I managed to piece together a pretty good picture of what our family life must have been like at the time I was born, seen through the eyes of the social workers who visited us and made the decisions about whether or not we should stay with our parents. They were there to assess us and they committed many of their judgements to paper.

For some people the responsibility of bringing up children is simply too much for them to be able to cope with, they just don't know where to start and can't be bothered to find out. Child-rearing is hard for even the most stable and educated of people, so it is doubly hard for those who have no role models, no experience, no patience and no money for the task.

It's not all to do with poverty; there are plenty of poor people who work hard, make sacrifices and do a good job of bringing up their families. It's more to do with ignorance and selfishness, and our mum had both those traits in abundance.

In her defence, men didn't have much to do with bringing up kids in those days, especially babies, so all the responsibility of caring for us would have fallen on her shoulders. But she really didn't know where to start in looking after us. She didn't know how to feed us or clean us or dress us. She had no idea how to meet any of our basic needs and little interest in finding out. Comedians create comic characters like *Little Britain*'s Vicki Pollard from reality, basing them on girls like my mum who become mothers over and over again before they're even old enough to know how to look after themselves properly, let alone a string of demanding babies and toddlers.

If there is a strong family structure behind them, with aunts and grandmothers to help with advice and practical backup, then the kids born to girls like this have a chance of doing well and being happy. There was an extended family behind us to start with because we were living with Mum's mother in the first few months of my life, but there was still no stability. Not only did my parents have no settled home of their own, Mum was always leaving Dad for other men – 'playing around' as they used to call it at the time. The whole family set-up must have been chaotic from the start, because eventually they were all evicted from my grandmother's council house. To be evicted from a council house when you are already living on one of the roughest estates in the area takes some doing, but they managed it.

The fact that she didn't know how to look after babies didn't stop Mum from having plenty of us. After Jocky and I had been taken away she went on to have Irene, James, and Yvonne. Then she changed partners and took up with a man called Andrew Anderson while Dad was in prison, going on to have five more children with him. The Andersons and the Wilsons were almost like two different clans, co-existing uneasily in a patch of territory that would have been too small for one family, let alone two. Even though we had all come from Mum and sometimes all lived in the same house, we were never one big happy family; we were never really a family at all, just a collection of people trying to survive in any way they could.

No one has ever explained to me why it was that Jocky and I were the only ones to be taken off to children's homes while the rest of them were allowed to stay in Mum's chaotic care. The two or three times we were taken home from St Margaret's for trial periods we always ended up being whisked away again, rescued by the social workers while the rest of our brothers and sisters stayed as a family unit. It can't have been that we were more difficult than the others because Jocky was never any trouble to anyone, as far as I know, whereas James got into almost as much trouble as me later on. Maybe there just wasn't room in the care system for every child that needed help in our area at the time, but because Jocky and I had already become their responsibility the authorities stuck with us. Maybe it was all just a matter of paperwork and official red tape.

My researches have turned up files that tell me that before we were sent to Greenbanks Children's Home, Jocky and I were both admitted to Cameron Hospital in Windygates with serious cases of impetigo, a highly contagious skin infection. There must have been other things wrong with us as well because I'm told there was a real danger we could both have died. Because we were contagious the records say the hospital staff kept us in isolation for several weeks. That must have been when the social workers were first alerted to the fact that Mum might not be coping with us properly. Once they became involved they decided we shouldn't be returned home from the hospital but should be taken into care instead. Perhaps they thought we had caught the illnesses due to Mum's poor housekeeping and care of us; perhaps they thought our lives might actually be in danger if they returned us to our home.

There was something in the notes made by the social workers, which I discovered many years later, that talked about Mum being 'in desertion', so maybe she had abandoned us at that stage and was shacked up with another man. That would have been a good reason not to send us home, because I doubt if anyone would have expected poor old Dad to cope as a single father. If Mum had subsequently gone back to Dad while she was having Irene, James and Yvonne, the social services might have assumed it was OK to leave the new children there at home, but that to bring two older children back into the house would be too much for her to cope with.

I'd like to think there were meetings held and everyone put a lot of care and thought into what would be the best thing to do with us, but I suspect it wasn't as thought-through as that. I dare say the social services were as stretched then as they are today and did whatever was the least trouble for them. The Royal Scottish Society for the Prevention of Cruelty to Children (RSSPCC) were involved in having us taken away as well, so things must have been pretty bad.

The homes we were sent to, both Greenbanks and St Margaret's, were always cleaner and nicer than our own home. Mum never got round to changing the bedclothes or anything like that, everything was filthy, including us, and we always had head lice and skin complaints.

On a Friday night, in the rare weeks when Dad had a wage packet in his pocket, Mum would have to go down to the pub to find him and take it off him before he spent it all on drink. But she wasn't any more reliable than he was with money once it was in her pocket; she spent everything she could get her hands on going to the bingo. She was always stealing from shops for a bit of extra cash, even serving a couple of short prison sentences for it and for breaching her probation.

Family legend had it that Dad had come from a good family. His parents and brothers and sisters had never been in any sort of trouble, but I'm told he got into a lot of bother with the police himself when he was younger. I don't think he can have been all that good at being a crook because one night he and a friend broke into a pub and stole some money and a load of bottles of whisky and rum. I dare say they'd had a few drinks to muster their courage, and what Dad hadn't realised was that he had cut his hand on some glass while breaking in and had left a trail of blood back to his home for the police to follow. When they turned up at the house they found him in bed, trying to look innocent, like they'd just woken him up from a deep sleep. But when they asked him to get up there was a terrible clanking of bottles from underneath the bedclothes, which pretty much gave the game away. They locked him up for a few months for that. But he was obviously never going to be a big-time criminal mastermind, any more than the rest of the family.

It was 1954 when I was born in Buckhaven in Fife, and shortly after we moved to Kirkcaldy. At that time in Kirkcaldy there was virtually no steady work for people like Dad unless they were willing to go down the pits, which unsurprisingly he didn't fancy. Our family was by no means unusual, just about everyone in our area was living on social security benefits and handouts, stripped of their pride and given no reason to get up in the mornings or to stay out of the pubs at night. We always had to live in the roughest areas because we were such a big family. Four- or five-bedroom council houses were hard to come by, so you had to take whatever accommodation you were offered, especially when you had kids and no job. Inevitably it would be in the worst part of town, and we were surrounded by other people who were finding life difficult too.

Gordon Brown, who was born three years before me, also grew up in Kirkcaldy. In 2005 he became MP for Kirkcaldy and Cowdenbeath. The poverty and hardship that he saw around him in his home town must have been one of the reasons he became such a committed socialist. Adam Smith, the famous eighteenth-century Scottish economist who believed in a free economy and inspired politicians like Margaret Thatcher and now even features on the English £20 note, was another native of the town.

People on the estates around us had to live by their wits, making the best of whatever they could find or scrounge, whether it was from welfare handouts or ducking and diving around the pubs and streets. None of it seemed unusual to us as kids, just the way things were. When there was no money for the electricity meters we would burn candles and make toast in front of open fires. Dad would fiddle the meters as much as he could but it didn't always work. If we needed cash we had to sell something, usually something that had been nicked in the first place.

Lying around a broad curve of the north shore of the Firth of Forth, the grey stone town had been a busy port for centuries, and was once even a centre for the whaling industry. The castle harks back to the proud days of the Kingdom of Fife, when the area was a series of walled communities with names like Linktown, Sinclairtown, Pathead, Gallatown, Dysart and Kirkcaldy. There were fierce rivalries between the different communities and it is said that a boy who scaled a wall to court a girl from another sector was hanged for his treachery, like a real life Romeo and Juliet. Maybe that is why there are still so many fights in the bars at closing time on a Saturday night, bad blood travelling on down through the centuries.

There were also a number of coalmines in the vicinity. Kirkcaldy was the place where linoleum was first manufactured and was well known in the area as a market town. Each spring the Links Market would arrive, bringing with it a funfair that stretched for well over a mile. But by the time Mum and Dad were struggling to make a living and raise their family, all the industries that had historically fed the local economy had already been in decline for decades. There was still a bit of trade coming in and out of the harbour, mainly scrap metal and grain going out, wood pulp, wheat and maize coming back in. There would always be a few fishing boats bobbing on the tide but the town's former days of glory and prosperity were long gone. Nobody had any money and everyone had too many mouths to feed. My parents weren't the only ones who spent what little money they had on drink and gambling, it was the only escape people had from the grim, grey reality of their lives as poverty and hopelessness dragged their spirits further and further down. Drink gave them the opportunity to be happy for at least a few hours each day, even if it ended up making their problems a hundred times worse in the long run.

So neither Jocky nor I had that good a first footing in life, but a start like ours doesn't defeat everyone, some people use it as a springboard to great things. Jocky, for instance, never seemed to let anything really worry him as long as he was warm, well fed and comfortable. I have no way of knowing if he's carrying secrets from those early years that he doesn't want to share, or if he remembers even less than I do. Or maybe he really was spared the things that happened to me, and that was why he was able to go on to become one of the great Scottish working-class heroes of his generation, while I struggled in vain to stay afloat.

Chapter Three

The way Mum behaved with other men must have broken Dad's heart, because I know he went on loving her till the day he died. It didn't matter how badly she treated him, he could do nothing to escape his feelings for her. If he had only fallen in love with a different woman, someone who would have loved him back and shown him some loyalty and respect, his whole life would have been different and so, I guess, would mine. I suppose none of us can choose who we fall in love with; none of us can really predict how the people we meet today will change over the years. It's all a bit of a lottery. If you marry someone when you are teenagers, you're both going to be very different ten years later, especially if you have a house full of screaming children to look after and the worries of the world on your shoulders. We can't choose who our parents are either; all we can do is make the best of the ones we're born to.

Dad had joined the Merchant Navy after leaving school. Going to sea had meant being away from home for long stretches of time, and whenever he was at sea or in some foreign port he would constantly worry that Mum was playing around with other men back in Methil, where they were living at the time. It must have been torture, trapped on a ship for weeks or months on end, imagining what might be going on at home, maybe even in his own bedroom. Most of the time his worries were probably well founded, although I dare say he eventually became paranoid and suspected Mum of sleeping with every man who even looked at her across a crowded bar. Although he was obviously in love with her, such personal and emotional subjects were never talked about in our house. That would have shown an unacceptable level of sentimentality and softness. When you live in a hard world you have to show yourself to be as hard as the next man. I know it must have been tough for my dad because one time he became so desperate to get home to Mum that he dived off the side of a ship that he was serving on while it was in Methil Docks and swam back to dry land through the grimy waters. There was no way he could stay sane living with that level of anxiety, and he knew he was going to have to find a way to stay closer to home.

He tried to get local work after leaving the navy. He laboured at a brickworks for a while but found the heat of the kilns too much to bear and only ever went in two or three days a week. After that he mainly did itinerant farm work, like picking potatoes or raspberries, but that was only seasonal and brought in very little money. Mum would do it too sometimes, without telling the benefits people, to try to get some extra cash into the house.

Although she was stocky Mum was an attractive woman who enjoyed dressing sexily when she went out, wearing stockings and high heels, always putting on lots of make-up and lipstick, her hair nicely done. She liked to go out, to the bingo mainly, and she liked to have fun, which generally meant having a good time with other men.

For a while, when Dad came out of prison after Mum had left him for Anderson, he was actually given lodgings in the same house as them. I don't know how he could have stood being with them, watching the woman he loved with another man every day, being left out, being their inconvenient lodger. I guess he must have spent most of his time in the pub trying to avoid having to see them, drinking away the pain of Mum's rejection of him. Unbelievably, he stayed with them for two or three years, enduring what can only have been constant torment, then one night he must have cracked under the strain because there was a big fight.

Fights weren't unusual around the estate. When men have no work and no prospects they become frustrated and aggressive, wanting to assert themselves and salvage at least some male pride. If you add drink into the mix you have an explosive cocktail. Most of the men I knew were angry most of the time and looking for a fight with anyone they could goad into insulting them.

'Who're you looking at?' was a familiar battle cry in the pubs and bars most evenings, and the enquiry usually resulted in someone getting a battering.

I would guess Dad came back from the pub with too much liquor in him that night and couldn't take the humiliation a moment longer. Knowing her, Mum most likely started the fight; probably pushed him too far, belittled him once too often or started slapping him around, and finally his basically kind nature snapped. By all accounts the three of them then went at each other hammer and tongs and the row escalated to such a level that the police became involved, and Dad, since he was only the lodger and not the man of the house, was chucked out onto the street.

Even when he was found a place of his own by the council he never moved more than two hundred yards away from Mum and us, and always lived alone. I suppose it was better than having to actually live in the same house as Mum and her lover, but seeing her and his kids around the area day in and day out can't have been much easier. He never married again, just went to the local pubs for his company and entertainment.

Although I resented him forcing Dad out of the family, Andrew Anderson wasn't a bad stepdad. He was a quiet sort of a bloke, not a man to pick fights with anyone unless forced into a corner. Like Dad he would spend most of his time in the pub, mainly to get away from Mum and all the kids in the house I guess. Mum still had a terrible temper and the constant lack of money would bring on horrible mood swings and explosions of anger that arrived with little or no warning. She was fearless and thought nothing of punching or kicking anyone who got in her way, however strong they might be. She would often put Anderson out on the street when she was fed up with him and sometimes wouldn't let him back into the house for several days.

He wasn't a complete wimp and once or twice he gave her a slap before walking out, but he was no match for her really because she was happy to bite and scratch and do whatever she wanted in order to inflict maximum pain and win the fight. Over the years I took a few hidings from her myself so I know how strong she was, and how relentlessly she would keep battering away once her temper was lost. The worst hidings usually happened when I was older and I had been brought back home by the police after having been caught doing something wrong. I never even attempted to hit her back because that would have made her a hundred times angrier. She didn't care who saw her laying into us; she would even start on me while the policemen were still standing there, watching. Once they had to intervene to stop her doing me a serious injury.

'That's enough now, Mrs Anderson,' they warned, pulling her off me. She genuinely had no idea about what was enough, she was just furious with everyone and everything in her life and needed to take her anger out on someone, anyone within reach. Maybe that was why social services so often wanted to put me beyond her reach.

When they were still together Dad occasionally fought back against her and, unlike Anderson, he was strong enough to win when things got physical. If they started seriously laying into one another any of us kids in the house would run for cover, diving under the beds to get out of the way and staying there until the shouting and banging was all over and it was safe to emerge. None of us would have dared to intervene in the course of the battle in case we got caught in the crossfire. It wasn't as if we felt we had to come to Mum's defence. She wasn't some helpless victim of a violent man; she was well able to look after herself and was usually the one to start it. If we interfered we were likely to end up getting a beating from her as well.

I remember one time when I was staying at home for one of the trial periods, my teachers told Mum I'd been fighting at school. I probably had, although I can't remember the actual incident. To my surprise she didn't lay into me the moment I came through the door, but when Dad got home later that day she instructed him to give me a good hiding to teach me a lesson. I was shaking in my shoes. I was used to spontaneous explosions of temper and violence around the house, but this was more like the sort of ritual beatings that went on at school, which made it all the more frightening. The expectation of a beating is often worse than the actual event itself. With a face like thunder, Dad ordered me to go up to the bed-room, stamping up the stairs behind me, breathing heavily as he prepared to dole out the punishment. As he slammed the door behind us I sensed I was in for the thrashing of a lifetime.

'Lie down,' he roared, ripping his belt from the loops of his trousers. I couldn't stop trembling, knowing the belt had a nasty buckle and expecting his blows to hurt even more than the headmaster's leather strap. I lay on the bed, eyes tightly shut, holding my breath, terrified of what was about to hit me.

The first blow landed with a crash on the bed beside me, so close I could feel the wind from it, making the mattress jump beneath me. Then another blow, and another, all of them narrowly missing me. Getting into the swing of it, he then started to hit the walls, making an incredible noise.

'Start screaming,' he hissed under his breath.

With a feeling of relief flooding through me I realised what he was doing and together we proceeded to put on a show of him beating me to within an inch of my life, all for Mum's benefit as she listened downstairs. It felt great, him and me against her, and I loved him for that.

When Mum became pregnant with my brother James, a doctor suggested I should go home for the birth. For some reason they didn't think Jocky needed to do the same, maybe because he had settled in well at St Margaret's and didn't seem to be as vulnerable and emotionally damaged as me. Jocky and I were never close at that time, even though I would have liked to have been. I knew he would always stick up for me if I needed him to. He was my hero, but he didn't want me hanging around him all the time. We had different friends and different lives. Children could stay in St Margaret's until they were eighteen, so I was one of the youngest ones, always trying to play with the older kids and always being rebuffed. Jocky had his life there sorted. He was doing fine at schoolwork and was good at sports as well, he didn't need to have his younger brother hanging round his neck, trying to join in, embarrassing him. I dare say he was quite relieved to see the back of me for a while.

After a few months back home with Mum and Dad things began to deteriorate again and the social workers decided I should be returned yet again to St Margaret's. Why they thought it was all right to leave

Mum with the new baby if it wasn't all right for her to bring me up I will never understand.

When Jocky and I had been returned to St Margaret's after the first trial visit home, when I was still just four years old, I had found that the couple who had been running it before, Mr and Mrs Gibson, had been replaced by a man called David Murphy. He was now our 'housefather'. I already knew of Murphy because he had been working at the home as an assistant before we went away. Murphy had always been very friendly with Gibson, hanging about the house the whole time during his training period, so he was a familiar face, even though I didn't know much about him.

'Call me Uncle Dave,' he said with a broad smile as he welcomed Jocky and me back.

Chapter Four

Around this time I started to behave strangely. When we were first living at St Margaret's Jocky and I would attend Elie Primary School, and it was there that I had started stealing. It was the beginning of a pattern of behaviour that would continue for the best part of thirty-five years and I was never able to understand why I did it. It seemed as if I had two different voices inside my head, voices that spoke clearly to my young, impressionable self, like they were actually people in the room with me. One of them would be goading me on to do bad things while the other was trying to be my conscience and trying to save me from myself. As I got older the evil voice became stronger and cleverer and more persuasive. Once I was an adult and started drinking heavily, the voice of good sense began to lose all influence, but as a small child there must have been another reason that the evil voice so often held sway over my behaviour, leading me astray.

Lawyers working for Fife Council would later try to prove that being bad was part of my genetic make-up and nothing to do with anything that might have gone on in St Margaret's. They would suggest that I had grown up under the malign influence of my parents and siblings, with all their thieving ways. But I only spent about two of the first ten years of my life with my family, so it seems likely that whatever was going on at St Margaret's was more of an influence on me than whatever I witnessed at home.

Admittedly my dad was no saint. He went to prison two or three times that I know of for burgling local supermarkets and pubs, but I wouldn't have known anything about that at the time, so I can hardly blame his influence. His genes, maybe? It doesn't sound very likely, and if that was the case how come Jocky was never tempted to steal anything?

Something or someone had turned me into a thief

by the time I was five. In between classes I would be slipping away from the crowd in the playground and pinching sweets from the pockets of the other kids' coats in the cloakroom, and I was always getting found out. I don't think I was even trying to be subtle about it, so maybe I was asking to be caught, trying to draw attention to myself, trying to tell the adult world that there was something wrong with me and that I needed their help. If that was the case, they didn't seem to be getting the message. All they saw was a thief who needed to be beaten regularly so that he would realise the error of his ways.

The punishment for virtually every transgression in the school was getting the strap across your hands from the headmaster. The strap was at least half an inch thick with two long leather tongues. The headmaster would wrap one end around his hand in order to get a good grip and to ensure we felt the full force of the blows as they cracked down on our bare skin.

Some of the other kids were so brave they were able to hold their hands out and take their punishment for as long as they were told, biting back the tears. They would take six of the most forceful blows on their outstretched palms and not even cry, saving their tears until they were safely back in the cloakroom. But I never had that much courage. I would burst into uncontrollable sobs before the first blow had even fallen and would whip my hands behind my back, away from sight, as if that was going to stop the headmaster from going through with the punishment. Even though I was younger than a lot of the braver kids, I still hated myself for being such a coward. The headmaster would become infuriated with my hysterical outbursts and I would end up getting the lashes round my bare legs instead, which was probably more painful, but I just couldn't steel myself to take the punishment that I knew I deserved.

I would sob for several minutes once it was all over bar the stinging, trying to hide myself away from everyone until I was able to gain some control and think a little about whatever it was that I had done wrong. The others would call me names like 'sissy' because I couldn't hide my tears or my fear, and I hated the thought that they believed I was soft. The men in the world I had been born into might be violent and they might be criminal and they might be idle and they might be drinkers, but they were never soft.

St Margaret's kids were already at a disadvantage when we got to school, and we were used to getting teased by the other pupils who came from proper family homes. We always stood out because Murphy would insist we wore shorts to school, right up to the age of twelve. Even on the coldest days of the vicious Scottish winters, when the local kids were wrapped up in their sensible long trousers, we had our knees exposed to the elements, marked out as second-class citizens, as being different to the others. It was annoying and humiliating, but at the same time, for me, it was nice to have any uniform at all. Mum and Dad never bothered with school uniforms for any of their kids, just sending us in with whatever we had been wearing when we went to bed the night before, most of it ragged and dirty. In either case the other kids never missed any opportunities for taunting us. At Elie they were constantly reminding us we were 'orphans' and had no mothers or fathers, as if we were likely to forget. I would try to make them understand that I wasn't an orphan. I would stick up for Mum and Dad, always truly believing it would only be a few weeks before they came to get me and take me back home for good to be a permanent part of the family with my brothers and sisters.

I can't be quite sure why Murphy decided I needed to go to a psychiatric hospital when I was five but I guess it was partly to do with the stealing, and partly to do with the fact that I used to go into trance-like states sometimes, as if trying to escape from the real world and into my own head. I spent a full year in Ovenstone and I remember a lovely nurse called Anne who specifically looked after me. When you live in institutions you remember anyone who shows you even the smallest amount of kindness and affection, just as I imagine a starving man will remember the unexpected gift of a meal.

The hospital had a much more relaxed atmosphere than St Margaret's, I suppose because the staff realised they were dealing with children who were more vulnerable than most. At the end of the year the doctors said they couldn't find anything wrong with me apart from depression, which they said they could help me control with medication.

They put me onto the necessary medication and told me there was nothing more they needed to do for me. There were times as I grew up when I stopped taking the medication, usually because it was taken away from me by someone in authority, but without it I was prone to panic attacks, unable to get my breath properly when they struck, anxious about everything, terrified of some unknown, unquantifiable thing that was just waiting to happen to me. It wouldn't matter how much I told myself I was being illogical and foolish and that there was nothing for me to worry about, the fear would not relax its grip.

When Anne, the nurse, told me I was going to be discharged from Ovenstone I felt a surge of happiness, believing that I was going to be taken home to Mum and Dad again and given another chance to live as part of a normal family, because every small kid assumes their own family is normal. It felt like I had finished my sentence for whatever crimes I might have committed, proved I wasn't crazy or bad, and was finally going to be set free to live like everyone else.

But on the morning of my release, as I packed my bag and waited by my bed, Anne told me I wasn't going home just yet; that I was going back to St Margaret's and back to Elie Primary School. All my dreams came crashing down in a moment and I felt my heart was breaking. Terrified that I had done something wrong and might never be allowed to go back home again, I sobbed and sobbed. Anne put her arm around my shoulders and tried to comfort me, but nothing was going to make any difference. The decision had been taken and my fate was sealed. I was going to be delivered back to Murphy and even as I wept I had no idea how bad things were about to become.

Chapter Five

'Uncle Dave', as we had to call him, had an almost godlike position at St Margaret's. He had complete power to do whatever he wanted whenever he wanted, and every other adult involved in the local care system seemed to be happy to let him. I would imagine it's very hard to find enough good people to fill all the jobs which place a person in a position of care, and so when someone comes along who is totally dedicated, inspiring and imaginative and willing to work all hours, everyone else heaves a sigh of relief and lets them get on with it. There was no doubting that when it came to running a children's home Murphy was brilliant at his job.

He had undertaken a course in social work and had succeeded in winning the confidence of all the social workers he had been involved with, including the Gibsons and everyone else involved in the running of St Margaret's. He was also an ex-policeman, and policemen still received a great deal of respect in a community like Fife. Knowing that about him made everyone feel even more comfortable about his trustworthiness, as if he had proved himself simply by having worn the uniform. In those days people still looked up to the police. It was a time when the only policeman seen on television was Dixon of Dock Green, who was like everyone's favourite grandfather, a wise, fair, decent man. Authority figures were still taken at face value and there wasn't the same degree of suspicion and cynicism that there is today. Anyone who had been in the force was automatically assumed to be a good, upstanding, law-abiding person. Police officers, we all thought, never did anything wrong. If you add to that the fact that Murphy was completely willing to dedicate his whole life to the nurturing and developing of a group of children whose families did not want, or were not able, to take responsibility for them he looked like a pretty perfect hero, practically a modern-day saint, in fact.

I would suspect that even if the authorities who hired him had heard any alarm bells ringing at the backs of their minds due to the fact that he was unmarried and seemed to have no interest in women, they were quick to ignore them. Who would want to lose such a potentially valuable man over a suspicion that might prove to be groundless? Just because he wasn't married didn't automatically mean there was anything wrong with him. There had always been plenty of confirmed bachelors working in the education business; if they all suddenly fell under suspicion the whole system would collapse. Those were the sorts of arguments that were common at that time, a very different time to this. Murphy was very much a man of his time and profited greatly from it.

Having said all that, the authorities were occasionally forced to take action when the evidence against someone in their employment became too pressing and threatened to cause embarrassment. The Gibsons, I later discovered when I started researching the files and back copies of newspapers from the time, had themselves been sacked from St Margaret's, although the exact reasons for their going were left a little vague. Money had gone missing, it was alleged, and there was talk of abuse, although nothing seemed to get as far as going to court. These things were seldom talked about openly in those days, just hinted at, considered too appalling to actually put into words in polite society. Most decent people, I suspect, simply couldn't believe that such evil deeds really happened, so everyone was happy to let the authorities brush the whole business under the carpet as quickly as possible so they could stop thinking about it.

If the Gibsons had left St Margaret's under a dark cloud, that would have made the council all the more grateful that Murphy was there to step into their shoes, and all the more willing to let him run St Margaret's without interference.

At the time he took over the home Murphy must have been in his late twenties, not much more than a lad himself. He would only have been around ten years older than the oldest boys there, more like one of their own generation than part of the grown-up world. He was very striking: good-looking, self-confident, physically fit, well dressed and always immaculately groomed. Social workers were supposed to come and see us regularly and talk to us directly, but they never did. They would just turn up, have a cup of tea with Murphy, listen to whatever he had to tell them, see for themselves that he was doing a brilliant job of running the place, and then go away again, no doubt relieved that there was nothing for them to worry about. To be honest, even if they had talked to us children they probably wouldn't have found out anything, because none of us would have dared to speak out against Murphy. Children didn't speak out in front of adults in those days anyway, and certainly not children like us. Phrases like 'don't speak until spoken to' and 'children should be seen and not heard' were commonplace then, and we were as brainwashed by them as anyone else. So Murphy was left to do whatever he chose with the running of the home and the organising of activities, and he did it wonderfully.

He was great at sport, keeping himself in good shape, and organising a variety of games every day.

There didn't seem to be anything he couldn't do: football, wrestling, boxing, canoeing, fishing, cricket, swimming, snooker, table tennis; even pole vaulting, of which Jocky became school champion (an incredible thought when you look at the size he later grew to, but he was once quite skinny, before the darts lifestyle took a hold of him).

Murphy was expert at everything and encouraged us all to join in every game he devised. Sometimes we would just go down onto the beach and he would organise a spontaneous game of volleyball. It was like one long Outward Bound course for boys, a million miles from how we would have been filling our spare time after school if we had still been living on the council estate, loitering around the streets, waiting for our parents outside the pub or amusing ourselves with a bit of shoplifting or arson. He would arrange camping and caravanning holidays for us at weekends and during the school holidays, things that Mum and Dad would never have been able to provide. Whatever holidays he arranged, he always came too, seeming to enjoy the active life as much as we did, probably more than some of us. Jocky and I both thrived on all the exercise and stimulation and because of Murphy's encouragement I joined the Boys' Club, the Scouts and the Boys' Brigade, organisations I would have known nothing about if I had still been at home. He opened my eyes to all sort of possibilities and opportunities.

He was musical too, able to play and teach any instrument he picked up, whether it was a trumpet or a violin, a clarinet or a guitar. To us he seemed to be the most accomplished man in the world. I wanted to play the bagpipes and so he got me a chanter to learn on. I loved playing that chanter, so much so that over the years to come Murphy knew he could use it as one of his methods to control me, threatening to take it away as a punishment if I didn't do as he told me.

Although he did have a temper and would sometimes lash out at boys who annoyed him, he was nearly always kind and patient with me during the day. He would often hand out special perks like sweets, particularly to the five or six of us who were known as 'Murphy's Pets' because of the extra attention he lavished on us. There was nothing that unusual about his explosions of temper or the strictness with which he sometimes dealt with disobedience; that was the way most schoolteachers and authority figures behaved towards children in those days. We were used to it. We might not like it, particularly the boys who seemed to regularly annoy him, but we didn't think it unusual.

In most ways it was nice to have a grown-up who gave the impression of liking me. Although I wouldn't have thought about it rationally at that stage, I must have been feeling hurt and rejected by the way Mum and Dad were treating me, so anything 'Uncle Dave' did to make me feel special was very welcome. At the same time it was slightly embarrassing to be singled out, made to look like a teacher's pet to the others. No child likes to be seen as different, no one really wants to stand out too much from the crowd.

A lot of the other children seemed to want to pick on me, particularly when we were at school and away from Murphy's watchful eye. Maybe I annoyed the other St Margaret's boys because I was one of Murphy's Pets, or maybe it was because I was always willing to stick up for myself and the other boys in the school liked to watch me get riled, to see how far they could push me before I lashed out at them. It was never very far. I was always getting into fights at school, defending myself when the others picked on me or teased me for coming from a children's home and being an 'orphan'. They all knew that if they pressed the right buttons they could set me off on the warpath, which was sometimes seen as a bit of entertainment. Gradually, however, they learned that it was a dangerous game to light my fuse because I had very few inhibitions when it came to fighting.

The ones who didn't like me called me 'cowboy' because when I fought I would punch and kick violently, just as I'd seen actors like John Wayne do in the movies, while the others were still slapping and pinching one another like most kids do at that age. I guess I had learned from Mum, or inherited a bit of her battling spirit, maybe. I wasn't frightened of any of them; if they wanted a fight that was what they would get. It always led to me getting into trouble with Murphy because fighting was strictly prohibited at St Margaret's, unless it was in the boxing or wrestling ring. The boxing lessons Murphy had given us certainly helped to toughen us up and taught me that you shouldn't really fight unless it was under controlled conditions in a ring, but if someone wound me up I would lose all sense of reason and control and just go for them with my bare fists, regardless of the consequences. After a few years at Elie Primary School everyone started to leave me alone, knowing I would always be willing to have a go and might very well hurt them in the process.

Having Jocky around was always a support, even though he never actually did anything to help me. Just knowing I had a big brother to call on made some of the other bullies a little more careful about picking on me. But then Jocky moved on to Waid Academy, a secondary school in Anstruther, and I only had my own reputation as a scrapper to rely on to keep myself safe in the Elie school playground.

I always seemed to be in trouble for something at Elie; if it wasn't the stealing it was the fighting. Although I always gave as good as I got, I was hardly ever the one who started the fights; but nine times out of ten I seemed to end up being the one hauled up in front of the headmaster, having to face the strap yet again. Maybe it was because, like Mum, I didn't care who saw me fighting and I would keep going till I was ready to stop, so I would often still be laying into someone when everyone else had spotted a member of staff approaching and had pulled back. Despite my willingness to get stuck in with my fists, I still couldn't find the courage to hold my hands out and take the strap like a man, and still ended up being lashed around the legs instead as I danced around, screaming blue murder.

I did eventually make some good friends amongst the other boys of my own age at St Margaret's, but the ones I befriended would often leave to live with foster parents as they got older, while I never seemed to go anywhere. I didn't envy them, because I didn't think I wanted to be fostered by some strange family, I just wanted to go home to my own mum and dad, but I missed them when they had gone. I don't know if Jocky and I were being offered for fostering, but if we were I guess we were being offered up as a package, making it harder to find anyone willing to take us on, or maybe my reputation as a 'bad boy' was travelling ahead of me and potential foster parents decided against taking the risk.

One couple did take us out one weekend, but they told the social workers they didn't want to keep us because what they really wanted was a girl. If you have set your heart on a sweet little girl, two rather boisterous boys, one of whom has a tendency for getting himself into trouble, are not going to be very appealing. I was really disappointed that time because I had liked them. As a sort of compensation they said they would be willing to take us away on holidays with them from time to time. It was a kind thought, softening the blow of yet another rejection, but it never happened. There are a lot of people in the world whose hearts are in the right place, but who never quite get round to putting their best intentions into practice. I suppose that is how someone like Murphy manages to get so far into the system; everyone is always happy to delegate the dirty work to someone else, particularly if that someone else shows themselves to be good at it. People just kept giving him children to look after because then their own consciences were clear.

Murphy was very strict about keeping the boys and the girls separate at St Margaret's. I don't know if that was because he was afraid the older ones would get up to no good, or whether he thought he could rule the boys better if he kept them apart. In those days, long before the 'sexual revolution' reached the edges of Scotland, birth control was pretty much unheard of and sex outside marriage still a terrible sin. So it was considered quite normal to keep the sexes totally segregated, unlike today where boys and girls are encouraged to mix from an early age, most of them becoming more balanced and mature as a result. Murphy didn't seem to have any interest in the girls at all, happy to leave their care to the women on the staff.

I must have missed having any female input in my life. All the games and activities that Murphy organised were great, but sometimes I felt like doing something gentler, more creative and imaginative perhaps. If I had been living at home I would have had my mother and my sisters to play with, as well as the other girls on the estate, but at St Margaret's such things were deeply frowned upon.

There was a chalet in the grounds which was only for the girls to play in, and strictly out of bounds for the boys. I knew it was forbidden but I couldn't resist sneaking in there on my own when I had no one to play with, to mess around with the dolls' houses, rearranging the furniture and disappearing into my own imaginary world. Murphy must have been following me around all the time because he always seemed to pop up whenever I was doing something wrong. Every time I slipped into the chalet I would become absorbed in my imaginary games and not hear him approaching until it was too late. Every time I was caught I had to be punished, regardless of whether I was one of Murphy's Pets or not.

His favourite punishment was to make us stand on the freezing cold bathroom tiles for two or three hours at night, bare-footed and wearing only our pyjama tops. One boy later remembered being made to stay there till four in the morning. I don't remember it being quite that late, but then he was one of the boys that Murphy seemed unable to resist picking on. Standing still for that long would be hard for anyone, but for a small boy who just wanted to curl up in his bed and go to sleep, the hours would seem to drag on for ever.

At other times he would order me to go to my room during the afternoon, forbidding me to look out the window, but knowing that I wouldn't be able to resist. I would stand forlornly behind the curtains, peeping out at all the others as they played in the garden or on the beach, having fun while I was trapped indoors on my own, watching the minutes tick past so slowly I feared I might go mad.

The girls at St Margaret's were looked after by Auntie Margaret, but there was no doubt that she was only a deputy to Murphy. He was the one with the overall power. She stayed most nights in a room in a converted attic at the top of the house. On the nights she was off duty other members of staff would sleep over in another room situated between the dormitories. Murphy's own room was downstairs in the basement at the other end of the big, rambling old house. There were three or four other staff, plus a cook and cleaners, none of whom lived in as far as I can remember.

There were four dormitories in the house, one big one for the girls and three for the boys, with around four boys sleeping in each. I often wet the bed and sometimes Auntie Margaret would be there to sort me out. Occasionally, when she had finished changing the sheets, she would see that I was looking so sad and frightened and tired, pining for my mother like a little lost puppy, that she would take me up to her attic room and let me tuck up into bed beside her, cuddling me as we fell asleep together in the warmth. I never wanted those nights to end.

It must have been obvious to her how lost and unhappy I was and how much I needed to be loved. She was a lovely woman and many, many years later I was touched to discover she had kept photographs of me. She probably assumed I was unhappy because I was so young to be away from my mother and she did her best to be a replacement, even though I wasn't really her responsibility.

She knew I had a tendency to steal things because one day she caught me helping myself to coal from the boiler house and solemnly stacking it away in a hiding place near the front door.

'What did you want the coal for?' she asked me afterwards, obviously puzzled as to why a small boy would be stockpiling fuel.

'I want to give it to my mum when she comes to see me,' I replied, 'to take home with her to keep her nice and warm.'

She gave me a bit of a ticking-off, but I don't think her heart can have been in it, and she didn't tell on me to Murphy.

Mum almost never came to see us and I'm sure Auntie Margaret was as aware of that fact as I was. Twice a year Mum would arrive for a visit, staying for only a few hours. She, Jocky and I would walk along the beach together just outside the house, with me tightly holding her hand, never wanting to let go. I would secretly long for us to keep walking, just the three of us, until the home had disappeared from view. But all too soon Mum would become bored with our childish company and start saying we needed to turn back, 'otherwise I'll miss the last bus'. She was probably worried about getting back home in time to get herself ready to go to the bingo. So she would leave us yet again, shattering my fantasies of her gathering us up in her arms to take us home and, after I'd waved her off, I would know that I had to start pinning my hopes on some new promise of a future date when she would be back to get us. The moment she had gone, Jocky would be straight back amongst his friends, apparently perfectly contented and accepting of the way things were, while I sank back into my own sad little dream world, wishing things could be different.

I have no memory of Dad ever visiting us at St Margaret's, and I don't think either Jocky or I would have expected him to. It just wasn't something that would have occurred to him.

Although I knew life was hard at home, that was still where I wanted to be. I wanted to be with my mum and dad, living amongst my other brothers and sisters. I didn't care if all I got to eat for my tea was a slice of bread and margarine, sprinkled with sugar to help it go down if there wasn't any jam – which was what usually happened. I would have been happy with whatever they could give me. I just wanted them to want me. It wasn't that Mum couldn't produce good food when she chose to, and when she had anything in the house to give us. She would some-times cook hearty soups or treat us to home-made chips, but five or six nights a week she would be out at bingo even when we were at home, and didn't want to be bothered with preparing meals for the family before she went.

Whenever she did come to visit us at St Margaret's she was always making promises. 'It won't be long now till we have you back home.'

Ninety per cent of me always believed that I would soon be out of St Margaret's and back home. I think all children start out believing everything their parents tell them. No one wants to think that their mother is a liar, any more than they want to believe that their mother doesn't want them. All small children make excuses for their parents long after the parents have exposed their inadequacies for all the world to see. If a parent chooses to make a lot of false promises to their child they will nearly always get away with it for a time. But the price they pay when the child finally accepts the truth will usually be terrible, because once the trust has gone they will never be able to win it back. Not that any of this would have concerned Mum. She couldn't have cared less whether we trusted her. For all I know she might even have believed her own words at the time. Most of her life was so grim she must have been living in a world of fantasy at least part of every day just to survive.

The beach became an important part of my private and solitary world. The back gate at St Margaret's led directly onto the sand and I was always escaping out there on my own whenever Murphy took his eye off me, lying in the dips between the sand dunes, sheltered from the world by the tufts of thick, wind- and salt-coarsened grass. I would stare up at the sun until my eyes began to play tricks on me, fading the world around me out in a glaze of light as I listened to the mournful cries of the seagulls circling above me in the sky and the roar of the sea far away across the sands, lost for two or three hours at a time in a blissful, daydreaming state.

I liked being on my own with nature, not having to deal with the demands of other people, their questions and their jibes, their instructions and their anger. The gulls and the waves made no demands on me, allowing my thoughts to circle round and round in my head: why was I like I was? Why did I steal things? Why couldn't I be like the other boys? Why didn't they do the things I did? How come Jocky was doing so well and seemed so settled and happy and resigned to his life in care? Why didn't my mum and dad want me?

No answers would come to any of the questions, but my thoughts would spiral away inside my head, allowing me to escape from the reality of the home and the school and the trouble I always seemed to be in.

Every time the staff realised I had gone missing again, usually after a couple of hours, they would send the other boys out to look for me, all of them combing the sands shouting out my name against the sounds of the wind and waves, but I would never hear them. Nothing going on around me could penetrate those daydreams; it was like I had entered another world. When the others eventually found me they would have to shake me back to consciousness, even though I wasn't asleep, just travelling to my own private reality somewhere deep inside my head.

Although I was one of Murphy's Pets, like everyone else I was subject to certain rules, such as the one about staying out of the girls' chalet, that he enforced ruthlessly. They had their own cook at St Margaret's and the food was good and plentiful considering the home must have been on a tight budget, but Murphy was completely inflexible about making us eat up anything we had asked for. I suppose his was the last generation to have experienced rationing and wartime shortages, when every scrap of food needed to be used up and nothing wasted.

There was one meal that remains forever fixed in my memory. Until that day I had never been given rice with meat or curry or anything like that; I'd only ever had bread or potatoes. In Scottish homes in those days rice was still only really used to make sweet rice pudding. The first time I saw it being served up as a main course at St Margaret's I was excited, thinking it would taste the same as the rice pudding that I liked. I eagerly held my plate out when Murphy asked who would like an extra helping.

As soon as I tasted it I realised it was something else entirely unlike rice pudding, and the texture of it turned my stomach. I didn't eat any more, pushing it to the side and picking at just the meat instead. At the end of the meal my plate was still heaped up with the untouched rice.

'You're gonna eat that rice, laddie,' Murphy warned me threateningly when he saw that I'd stopped.

'I don't like the taste of it,' I explained. 'I thought it was like that other rice.'

But he wasn't having any of it and made me sit at that table until every mouthful had gone. I can still remember the taste of it as I turned it over and over in my mouth, the mound on the plate in front of me stubbornly refusing to grow any smaller while I gagged over every swallow. Even when I vomited over the plate he refused to allow me to give up. It must have taken three hours to get through it and to this day I can't eat rice without the smell and taste of that meal coming back to haunt me.

It's funny how such small things can stick in the memory, when I was later able to temporarily forget so many far worse things. The human brain is strangely selective about what it retains, possibly to protect itself from the unbearable memories.

Chapter Six

When I was six years old the social workers decided that Mum and Dad should be given another chance at looking after us, and Jocky and I were taken home once more for another trial period. I was so happy to be home, it was what I had been longing for every day and night since I'd been sent back to St Margaret's, but it was still hard to cope with Mum's temper and there wasn't much space for me to get away from everyone and daydream. Most nights we were having to sleep four or five to a bed just to fit us all in the house at the same time. Our living standards generally took a bit of getting used to. In St Margaret's the 'aunties', like Auntie Margaret, kept everything clean and tidy and organised, but Mum and Dad could never be bothered with any of that. When you are a small child it is reassuring to think that the adults who are in charge of you are capable of controlling things. You want to feel you can rely on them to protect you whatever might happen. Auntie Margaret was that sort of person, and in most ways so was Murphy; Mum definitely was not.

When I was away from my brothers and sisters I longed so much to be with them at home that it was like a physical ache, but the reality of us all living together was never as much fun as I had hoped. I don't know quite what I expected, but it always felt disappointing. Maybe I imagined a big welcome home with people telling me how much they had missed me and how good it was to have me back. Instead they more or less ignored me, just getting on with their lives and leaving me to settle back in as best I could. I was used to living amongst a lot of other people, so I was OK with it, but it still wasn't the sort of homecoming I had fantasised about.

In fairness to them, I must have been like a stranger to my younger brothers and sisters. They weren't used to having me around and didn't know how to fit me into their routines, how to include me in the relationships they all had with one another. I felt I was an outsider intruding on their family life, when all I wanted was to feel like they were *my* family. It was as if I was sitting on the sidelines just watching their daily life going by, like when I sometimes sat and watched people picnicking on the beach outside St Margaret's and wished that they were my family.

None of it was surprising, now that I look back with the wisdom of age, but at the time I felt rejected and hurt and unsure of where I fitted in. My brothers and sisters had grown up together but they were like strangers to me, and by then I was already too damaged to be able to make the necessary adjustment successfully. I dare say I was moody and difficult to live with, but I never felt that I was loved and I knew that I didn't love them either. Jocky didn't seem to have any problems fitting in, wherever he was he just got on with things, with just being himself. I wished I could be more like him, but I couldn't work out how to do it or what his secret was.

I never spoke about any of these feelings to anyone;

73

I wouldn't have known what words to use, but it was all going on inside my damaged little head, fermenting in a dark, resentful, puzzled silence. It would be many years before anyone found the key to help me let all that stockpiled anger out, by which time the damage had already been done.

The social services left Jocky and me with Mum and Dad for an entire year and then decided, without giving us any warning, that their experiment wasn't working and that we were once more at risk. Mum and Dad, it seemed, had failed yet again to convince the authorities that they were fit parents. A hit squad of social workers turned up at the door unannounced one day and attempted to bundle Jocky and me into the back of a car in order to whisk us back to St Margaret's, saving us from some danger at home which they had decided was suddenly grave and imminent. Shocked and heartbroken at being taken away again, I was kicking and screaming and crying as they tried to get me out of the house. I was sure that I must have done something wrong that I was going to be punished for, because I was always being told how bad I was. Why else would they be taking me away from my mum if it wasn't because I was a naughty boy? But I didn't want to ask anyone what I had done in case it reminded them that I deserved a beating.

In my heart of hearts I knew I hadn't been very kind to next door's cat (which is surprising, looking back now, considering how much I have loved animals as an adult. Maybe I was just pleased to find something weaker than me that I could take out some of my frustration on), and I thought perhaps that was why I was being punished. But then I couldn't imagine what Jocky could have done, because he never did anything wrong as far as I knew. So why was he being taken back as well? None of it made sense and no one was even trying to explain. All I can remember is that there was a lot of shouting and arguing and pushing.

Of course in the end it didn't matter how hard I fought to stay out of the car, I knew they would take me eventually because other people always did whatever they wanted with us in the end. No doubt I put up a better fight than I had the last time, when I was even smaller, but I was still only seven years old and no match for the strength of determined adults. There was no way they were going to change their minds just because I didn't want to go. It would never have occurred to them that I might have an opinion on where I should be allowed to live; they were the professionals and so they 'knew best'. But then again maybe they did know things that I didn't, things that adults understood but were quite outside my realm of comprehension.

Since Mum and Dad made no effort to help me fight off these intruders into our family, who seemed to me to be virtually kidnapping us in broad daylight, I suppose they must have been in agreement that we would be better off back in a children's home. Their placidity was a puzzle too. I couldn't understand why they wouldn't want to keep us like they kept all the others. Why weren't they fighting for us? Why were we any different?

Years later, when I got access to the social services files for the case, I saw it written down in black and white that the social workers concerned had decided, after leaving us there for a year's trial, that 'Mr and Mrs Wilson were not proper parents'. It seemed odd to see something so personal stated so boldly like that. Because we had only been allowed home on trial we were still under the council's care and they could do what they pleased with us without having to go back to the courts. It seems amazing that they allowed us to stay there for a full year if they were so concerned about our welfare, and even more surprising that they didn't think it would be upsetting for us to be uprooted again. A year is a long time in a small child's life and however unsatisfactory the family situation might have been, it had still become our home once more.

The other surprising thing is that during that year I caused virtually no trouble at my new school. The teachers reported that I was occasionally a bit late coming into class, but there was no mention of stealing or of any disruptive behaviour and I certainly have no memory of doing anything wrong while I was there. It had only been at Elie Primary School that the stealing and fighting incidents happened, while I was living at St Margaret's. It must have been something there that was upsetting me, making me act irrationally, and now I was on my way back there.

*

Murphy welcomed me back to St Margaret's as if he really meant it. Just like the previous times I'd returned from trial periods at home and when I first got back from Ovenstone, he was very nice to me, giving me extra sweets and treats. Like all the boys, I was totally in awe of him because in truth he was the closest thing I'd ever had to a father figure. I loved Dad, but even when I was living at home he was hardly ever around and he paid none of his children any more attention than he had to. I can remember him occasionally sitting me on his lap if he came in from the pub in a good mood, but he would soon lose interest with my silly nonsense and push me aside to have his tea or watch the television or have a fight with Mum. There was no way Dad would have gone to the trouble of organising a game of football for me, or taken me on a camping trip, or out in a sailing boat. He wouldn't have known how to begin to arrange such things. In those ways Murphy was almost like a fantasy father, the sort of man that little boys would like to imagine their fathers to be, even when they blatantly aren't. With Murphy I felt my life was in safe hands, even if I would rather have been back at home.

So the first time he lifted me from my bed while I was asleep I thought he would just be taking me for a cuddle like the ones I got from Auntie Margaret, and I snuggled sleepily into his broad chest, feeling safe in his strong arms as he carried me along the cold corridor to his basement room. I was sad and lonely and welcomed the promise of a fatherly cuddle. While the other children slept on in their dormitories, oblivious to what was happening to me, he carried me silently down the stairs to his bedroom, like a huntsman taking home a trophy kill to devour in private.

It was quite comforting in my half-awake state as he slid me into his bed, stroked my face and kissed my neck. It tickled a bit and made me squirm but it wasn't unpleasant. Then he undid the buttons of my pyjama jacket and stroked my chest. Sliding his hand down he slipped my pyjama trousers down my legs and off over my feet. Then he climbed between the sheets beside me, both of us now naked.

Suddenly I was fully awake, some invisible alarm bell sounding in my head, unable to work out what was happening or what was expected of me. Why was

I naked? What was he going to do? I don't think I felt exactly afraid because I still trusted him at that stage; I was more puzzled and apprehensive, anxious to do the right thing and not upset him. But I remember desperately wanting to put my trousers back on, feeling awkward and vulnerable without any clothes.

His room was small and dark, not much wider than the double bed that took up most of the floor space, leaving only enough room for a wardrobe and a table. The air smelled strongly of his aftershave and the Brylcreem he applied each day to his hair. Like many good-looking men, he was vain and took a lot of care in his appearance, always brushing his teeth and showing off his muscles to us.

None of what he was doing that night was that unpleasant and he wasn't hurting me physically in any way, but something told me I was entering a new world that might hold dangers I couldn't yet imagine. I stayed as still as I could, holding my breath, letting him do whatever he wanted, waiting to see what would happen next, hoping it would all be over soon.

There was one window in the room, which looked out over the sea, like so many of the windows at St

Margaret's, and I could hear the waves crashing down on the dark shore outside.

To start with he was very gentle and loving and I had no idea what he was doing, or that it was wrong when he pushed his tongue into my ear. Nothing too terrible happened that night and after a while he carried me back up to my room and tucked me up in my own bed as quietly as he had lifted me. The whole interlude was so strange that in the morning it almost felt like I had dreamt it. But a few nights later it happened again. I didn't dare protest this time either, but I didn't want to go with him. I wanted to be warm and asleep in my own little nest, not being spirited around the cold, unlit, night-time corridors of St Margaret's.

Each night he came for me after that he became a little rougher with me, making more demands, seeming to want to hurt me, or at least certainly not caring if he did. He made me touch his penis and masturbate him which was horrible, then started pinning me down on the bed and forcing me to do things that hurt and frightened me, covering my head with a pillow to stifle the sounds when I cried out in fear and pain. He would press down so hard I was sure I would suffocate. Eventually I would have to give in and fall quiet to conserve the air in my lungs as I struggled to find a way to turn my head that would allow me to breathe again. It was so terrifying and as I concentrated all my energies on struggling to stay alive under the pillow I became less aware of what he was doing to the rest of me.

He forced me to put his penis in my mouth too, which made me gag like I was going to be sick. I can't have been doing it right for him because he only tried that three or four times before giving up. He soon moved on to other things, turning me over, holding me in a grip of iron, pulling me into him, forcing his penis into my backside, making me cry out with the pain. Even if he hadn't smothered my face with the pillow, no one would have heard my cries anyway; his room was a long way from the dormitories and at the other end of the house from Auntie Margaret, who was sleeping soundly in her own bed, oblivious of the evil deeds going on below her.

I didn't like what was happening to me, but I didn't think I had any option other than to let him do whatever he chose. After all, I didn't like being taken from my parents, but no amount of fighting and pleading had stopped that. To start with I didn't even realise that he wasn't allowed to do whatever he wanted to me. He was the adult, after all, the 'Uncle Dave' that everyone looked up to, so he must know the right thing to do. But if it was the right thing, then why did it hurt so much? And why did I feel so bad? I felt like I was no more than a piece of meat that he could do whatever he wanted with, I wasn't Tommy, I wasn't even a child, just an object. It seemed like he didn't care about me as a person at all. I wasn't Murphy's Pet after all; I was more like his toy.

I had been living in institutions most of my life, deprived of any privacy, and even in the times when I went home there were always other people in every room. The only thing that was private was my own body and whatever went on in my head. But now Murphy was invading these internal places too, penetrating my body and entering my nightmares. Because of him there was nowhere left for me to hide away from the world and be on my own. He had robbed me of my last shreds of privacy, dignity and peace.

When he had finished with me in the night he would carry me back to the dormitory again, creeping up through the house with me in his arms, careful not to wake anyone on the way, sliding me back between my own sheets, which were still rumpled from where I had been lying before he took me but had grown cold in my absence. As soon as I was safely under my own blankets I would curl up into a ball, cowering away as he crept out of the room and vanished again into the silent darkness, crying myself to sleep, aware that I had no one to help me, no one who would believe me. I wasn't even sure that I deserved help. Had I brought this on myself by being so bad? Was this just the way things were for a boy like me?

I didn't start to question his right to pluck me from my bed whenever he wanted for many years, not until I was around eleven years old. And even then I didn't know how to stop him from doing whatever he wanted. Any protest I made would seem feeble in the shadow of his confidence in his own power to rule me absolutely. If I protested he just mocked my pathetic attempts to assert myself, brushing them aside. All I could really do was sulk and brood and be less than co-operative around the home. It was like he was all-powerful within the walls of St Margaret's, like some Third World dictator who can demand whatever he wants from his people, having them killed or imprisoned for even thinking about opposing him, or bringing them to his bed whenever he felt the urge.

He never took me from my bed two nights in a row. Sometimes there might even be a week or two between his visits and I would never know as I lay there, waiting to go to sleep, if this would be a night he would arrive and scoop me up or not. It wouldn't be until I woke up in the morning that I would know I had been allowed to sleep undisturbed and then I would start to worry about what might happen the following night.

It was only many years later that I learnt that those gaps between his visits happened because he had several other favourite Murphy's Pets, and he would rotate us on different nights. There is really no way of knowing how many of us he was using each day. One victim has recently gone on record as saying he thinks it might have been as many as two or three a day, but having studied all the evidence and listened to all the testimonies, I think it was probably more like one of us every two or three days. So at least two or three times a week he would be taking someone to pleasure himself with, while we all thought we were the only ones suffering and didn't dare breathe a word about it to anyone else. Maybe if we had known we weren't alone we would have found the strength to stand up to him, but I doubt if we would even have done that, so great was his power over us.

'I want to be like a father to you, Tommy,' he would say when he was trying to win me over from a sulk. 'Wouldn't you like that?'

'No,' I would snap, quite confident in my defiance when he was trying to ingratiate himself in that way.

It wasn't true, I would have liked him to be my dad in many respects, but I knew that no father should be doing what he was doing to me in his bedroom. If it hadn't been for the abuse I would have idolised him completely, just as so many other people did who knew nothing about the secret, dark side of his character.

'Nobody loves you,' he would taunt me when he

wanted to convince me that I should be grateful for the attention he was paying me. 'Nobody wants you. Your mum doesn't love you. I'm the only one who cares about you.'

It was easy to believe him when he said that, because the evidence was there every time Mum and Dad let me down by failing to turn up when they promised. Murphy would sometimes tell me in the morning that they were coming to see me and I would go running upstairs to get changed and washed, excitedly planning the day ahead, wondering if this would be the time they kept their promise and took us home with them. I would come down a little later and he would be waiting for me with a look of mock sympathy on his face.

'Oh,' he'd say, 'there's been a phone call, Tommy. You're not getting a visit today after all. Your mum and dad can't come.'

Then he'd stroll off, leaving me alone as I sat crying by the front door. It was his way of making himself seem like a better parent to me than my own mum and dad. What I didn't realise until years later was that often he had rung them and told them not to come, making up some excuse about me being away on a camping holiday. Maybe it was even true, because we did go on a lot of those trips, where he would be the only adult in charge of us, leaving him able to do whatever he wanted to us under the cover of darkness.

I already believed Mum didn't care about me most of the time because she was always letting me down, even without Murphy's interference. She would be promising me she would come or, when she did come, she would be promising that I could go home soon; but it never happened. I always blamed her rather than my father for the fact that I was put into a home and for everything that was allowed to happen to me there. In my old-fashioned little mind it wasn't really Dad's job to look after us as the man of the family, it was hers. He wasn't the one who was always shouting at us and hitting us. I'm sure he played his part in the whole mess of our childhoods but to my young brain, which saw things pretty starkly in black and white, Mum was the one to shoulder the bulk of the blame.

Having discovered that he could get away with

almost anything, Murphy became bolder and started taking me into his room during the day sometimes as well, for kissing sessions. I hated it so much, but there was no way I could disobey him, so I would take my revenge in subtler ways. He had a biscuit tin in his wardrobe, which he would put all his loose change into until it was almost full with coins. Once I had discovered it was there I would wait for the right opportunity to pilfer from it. It was a small victory and didn't make me feel any better, in fact it usually made me feel guilty for stealing, only adding to and worsening all the other emotions boiling up inside me. I'm sure he must have known that I was doing it, but he probably thought it was a price worth paying.

The first time he penetrated my backside fully I was still at primary school and I must have been about eight years old. I know that for sure because I can remember how sore my bottom was when I went into school the next day, so sore that I wasn't able to sit down on the hard classroom chair. The teacher, tired of continually telling me to sit down and stay still, mistook my wriggling and fidgeting around for bad behaviour and I was sent in front of the headmaster to receive the strap yet again for being disruptive and disobedient. I wanted to tell him that it wasn't my fault but it wasn't something I could talk about easily, and anyway in my heart I knew he wouldn't have believed me.

The first few times Murphy penetrated me the pain was intense, like I was being torn apart, and I couldn't stop myself from screaming and struggling to escape. But he was a strong man and once his huge, rough hands had a grip of me there was no getting away until he was ready to release me, however hard I fought. It was the same when he joined in the wrestling sessions with us during the day, pinning us to the floor, rubbing himself against us as we wriggled around beneath him in vain, no doubt inflaming his desires even further with our attempts to escape. At the time we all assumed that was part of the sport, the way it should be taught. We wanted to learn the right way to do it because we all wanted to be tough guys, to be able to look after ourselves in a fight. Only looking back as an adult can I see how much it must have been to his taste to be rolling around on the floor with us. Indulging in those sorts of activities during the day must have left him frustrated and aroused by the time the nights came, driving him to look for relief wherever he could find it.

There were other part-time staff coming and going in the home. I remember 'Uncle Tom', an Irishman, who lived there while he was on a social worker's course. He had a bedroom next to Murphy's. He used to grab me as I tried to run past, lift me off the ground and rub his bristly chin against my face, which I hated because it made me sore. He said he was just being 'playful', but it didn't seem like play to me although I didn't really understand what it was. He was older than Murphy and not in such good shape. His breath used to smell too, which Murphy's never would because he was so fanatical about health and hygiene, never smoking or drinking.

I remember Uncle Tom getting his penis out one day when no one else was around and trying to persuade me to play with it. I refused because he was the sort of man you could stand up to, not like Murphy whom no child dared defy. I told him that if he did it one more time I would tell the village bobby, who used to travel around the place on a pushbike, a bit like a character from a children's story. To my surprise and relief he actually believed me and didn't try it on again. By that stage I must have worked out that the grown-ups weren't allowed to do things like that, otherwise I wouldn't have known to threaten him with the police. Uncle Tom disappeared back to Ireland and many years later got charged with abusing us, but he was in poor mental health by then and was secluded in a psychiatric hospital. The police held out little hope of being able to get to him and I don't think he ever had to stand trial. I'm sure he must be dead by now.

Everything seemed to be going wrong inside my head by then. I just couldn't understand what was going on or why I was having to live a life that made me so unhappy. I spent more and more of my time alone, lost in my own thoughts, disconnected from the real world, brewing up trouble for the future.

Chapter Seven

While everything inside my head was spinning out of control, Jocky just seemed to be completely grounded, getting on with life in the home; nothing much ever seemed to bother him. He never wanted to get involved with my life at St Margaret's and, until the day Murphy asked him to have a word with me, he never so much as expressed an opinion or attempted to stand up for me when I got into trouble. But on this particular occasion Murphy was threatening to send me away to the approved school and he wanted Jocky to talk me into apologising so I didn't have to go.

In fairness, Jocky had never had any reason to

interfere before that, since I gave him no clue that anything was going wrong or that I needed his help. He knew that I didn't pay attention at school or to those around me and got into trouble for nicking things, because everyone in the home knew about that, but he was used to his little brother being a bit of a headache to the staff; it wasn't his problem. Sometimes I was tagging along behind him and sometimes I wasn't, it was all the same to him by then. I never gave him any bother though. Why would I? He was my hero, after all.

But when I was eleven things got a bit more serious. I had been caught stealing again at school, from the headmaster's desk this time. I don't think I ever really stopped my campaign of pilfering, but this time it was thought I had finally overstepped the line. I had slipped back into the classroom during a break, when everyone else was outside playing, and taken half a crown (12.5 pence in today's money) from the headmaster's desk, along with a copy of my own school photograph which I wanted to give to Mum next time she visited. I have no idea why I did it. I didn't need the money and I guess I could have had the picture anyway if I'd asked for it, but I felt driven to be caught doing the wrong thing. My crime wasn't worth the effort and was bound to be discovered. I guess it had become the only way in which I knew I could get some attention, no matter how negative that attention was.

As well as giving me a hiding with the strap as soon as he'd worked out what I'd done, the headmaster notified Murphy immediately that I was up to my old tricks again and Murphy was waiting for me when I got back to St Margaret's that afternoon. I doubt that the headmaster realised quite how violently Murphy would react to this latest misdemeanour. He may also not have known that two or three weeks before the theft I had actually run away from St Margaret's, which was why Murphy was already angry with me even before he received news of my latest transgression.

It may have been that Murphy was also growing nervous that I was becoming too bold and wilful and might soon find the courage to speak out to someone in authority about the things he was doing to me in secret. I realise now that I was entirely dispensable to him because there were plenty of other, younger boys living at the home whom he could still intimidate into silence whilst he abused them. If I was likely to cause him a problem he would have wanted to nip it in the bud. His whole way of life depended on boys like me being too frightened to speak out – he must have known that one day someone might slip through his net of control and might actually be believed by the outside world. Although he seemed totally confident of his position, there must have been moments of fear when he felt that he could not afford to take any risks with a boy who was behaving like a loose cannon.

My escape from the home a few weeks before had been the first time I had ever run away, and I don't know why I chose that particular moment to do it. Perhaps the various pieces of my life were beginning to come together in my head like a jigsaw and I was realising that what was being done to me was wrong and that I shouldn't have to endure it a moment longer. Maybe I thought I was old enough to start making a few decisions of my own about how I wanted my life to be. There's always a stage in everyone's life when they realise they don't have to put up with anything that has been done to them as a child if they don't want to, that they can do something about it.

I'm sure I had lots of good reasons in my head as to why it was OK for me to just leave, but I also knew it was wrong to go; that I was still too young to be allowed to make my own decisions, that it wasn't allowed and that I would be breaking the rules. The same voice in my head that would instruct me to steal was urging me on to do it, to take some control of my own destiny, to just walk out the door and keep on walking and damn the consequences. My heart was thumping in my chest as I climbed on the bus to Kirkcaldy from outside St Margaret's, expecting at any moment to hear Murphy's angry voice shouting after me. No one on the bus took any notice of me, which felt nice, like I was just an ordinary boy going home in an ordinary way.

As the bus stopped and started and ground along on its journey my heart continued to thump, more now with excitement over what would happen next. It was such an easy journey to make that it was difficult to imagine why Mum and Dad had always found it so hard. If I could just hop on a bus to go and see them, why could they not have done the same to see me more often? I suppose everyone discovers their parents' failings bit by bit as they grow older themselves. I watched the other people getting on and off as we came closer to our destination; I was looking forward to the welcome I imagined I would receive from my family as I walked through the door. I could picture the surprise on Mum's face and the way they would want me to tell them about the journey and how they would tell me how brave and clever I was to do such a thing on my own.

When we reached Kirkcaldy I stepped off with a strange feeling of freedom, as if I had just travelled halfway around the world instead of ten or fifteen miles down the Scottish coast. I turned to walk home and bumped straight into my sister, Irene, who greeted me as if it were the most normal thing in the world for me to be getting off a bus in the town centre, and took me home to Mum. I was a bit annoyed that I wasn't going to be able to walk in on my own, demonstrating my independence for all to see.

I suppose I hoped that Mum, despite all the evidence I had seen in the past, was going to welcome me with open arms. I hoped that she would be so impressed that I had managed such a journey on my own, a journey which I knew she always found daunting, that she would listen to what I had to say and would see how unhappy I was and how much I wanted to come home. I must still have hoped she would want to protect me and look after me and would say that it was all right for me to stay with her and not go back.

Of course it was nothing like that and instead she got straight on the phone to the home and told them where I was, like I was some wild animal that had escaped from the zoo and might be a danger to the public. She obviously wanted to be rid of me as quickly as possible. I suppose I should have been thankful she didn't beat me black and blue like she usually did when I caused her inconvenience. I pleaded and cried but she wasn't having any of it. I dare say the more I cried the more she wanted to get me out of the house. It had been such a short-lived moment of freedom and I had to face the fact that I had been fooling myself if I thought I actually had any power over my own destiny.

Auntie Margaret took the phone call and came over to collect me an hour or two later, which was a relief as I was terrified of what Murphy would do to punish me and at least while I was with her I felt safe. It broke my heart yet again as we drove away in her car and I looked back to see that Mum had already gone inside and closed the door, as if I had never been there at all.

However kind and understanding Auntie Margaret might have been as she coaxed me into the car and chatted to me on the drive back, I knew Murphy would be furious with me for challenging his authority, for even suggesting that I might prefer to be with my real mum and dad instead of with him. He was always telling me they didn't love me and he would make out that I was being ungrateful for all he had done for me over the years by suggesting I wanted to go home to them. By running away I was saying that St Margaret's wasn't a wonderful place to be, that his little kingdom wasn't perfect.

The journey back in the car was a lot quicker than

the bus ride had been. When we drew up and Auntie Margaret walked in with me Murphy was waiting, and he was just as angry as I had expected, telling me over and over again that I was bad and warning me that I was on the verge of getting into such really big trouble that even he wouldn't be able to save me from it.

I had every reason to believe him and all his threats, so why did I slip that money and the photograph out of the headmaster's desk a few weeks later? I must have known I would be caught, because I nearly always was, and they only had to see which photograph was missing to make a guess at who the thief might be. Was I deliberately trying to show him that I wasn't afraid of him? Was I daring him to do his worst?

So Murphy was still angry with me for the running-home incident when the headmaster rang up to tell him about the stealing, and he had no trouble convincing me what a wicked boy I was the moment I walked in through the door from school, my legs still smarting from the strapping I'd received earlier. Each time I got into trouble he seemed to raise the level of his threats. When I was very tiny I could be cowed into a fearful submission just by his disapproval or by the threat of a removed privilege, and then he had to start inflicting the punishments like sending me to my room or making me stand for hours on the bathroom floor at bedtime. Now he was beginning to warn of other dire things he could inflict on me if I continued to be so disobedient and dishonest.

He was talking about the other people I would be handed over to if I became too disobedient for St Margaret's to handle; conjuring up images of terrible bogeymen in the hope that he would frighten me into obedience. He even threatened to tell the village bobby what I'd done. Since he was an ex-policeman himself I knew he wouldn't be frightened to do that, and assumed he would be listened to. I was sure he would be able to convince the bobby that he had my best interests at heart and was punishing me to try to stop me from going completely off the rails before it was too late. He always had a knack of making it sound like he was doing everything for our own good. Every punishment was somehow intended to help us stay on the straight and narrow, every hardship, he told us, was a deliberate attempt to toughen us up for the trials and tribulations that were bound to lie ahead of us on life's rocky road.

But I must have been growing a lot bolder because I remember refusing to let him intimidate me with a threat like that.

'If you tell the bobby,' I retorted, mustering all my courage, 'I'll tell him what you've been doing to me.'

I was just starting to realise that the things he did to me weren't right, that they might even be illegal, that maybe I didn't have to always do what he told me just because he was the housefather. Even if my shaking legs told me that standing up to him was a risk, I somehow found the courage to hold my ground. I knew I was wrong for stealing from the headmaster's desk, but the theft had been relatively trivial and Murphy's reaction of threatening to inform the police and suggesting he could have me sent to prison seemed out of all proportion.

I soon realised that standing up to him was a mistake. I thought I was calling his bluff, but it wasn't a bluff at all. When it came to my life and what could happen to me next, he really did have the controlling hand. There was no way he was going to allow me to threaten him that easily. I had gone a step too far and shown him what I might be capable of if he didn't do something about it. He wasted no time in dealing with me and the risk I presented. I was to leave St Margaret's. Murphy was sending me to a 'bad boys' school'.

In doing this Murphy was making sure that everyone knew just how out of control and bad I was, so it would be even less likely that I would be believed if I did ever tell tales on him at a later date. He was branding me as a troublemaker, making sure that it was clearly stated in my records that I was not someone to be trusted or believed.

'I'll tell them what you do to me,' I threatened again, becoming increasingly desperate as I realised my threats were not having the desired effect on him, using the only card I had to play in his high-stakes game of poker.

'You'll never be believed,' he sneered, and in my heart I knew he was right. Who would take my word, a known thief and unco-operative boy from a dysfunctional family, against someone who was an ex-policeman and known to do so much good work for the community and for dozens of ungrateful children just like me? They would think I was making it up to get myself out of trouble, to be vindictive towards a man who everyone else believed to be the best thing that had ever happened to me. Even if they did listen to me, how would I ever prove that what I was saying was true?

'You've been a liar all your life,' he kept up the humiliation, confident that he was winning, 'from the day you were born.'

He had told me I was a liar so often by then I was beginning to wonder if he was right; after all I knew I was a thief, but at the same time I knew that I always owned up as soon as I was caught. Didn't that mean that I wasn't a born liar? It was all so confusing, trying to work out in my head what was right and what was wrong. If Murphy was the one who was always right, how come he did such dreadful things to me? And he was the one who would be lying if he denied it to anyone else, which I knew he would, so that made him the liar, didn't it, not me?

In fact all my threats were empty, as he probably guessed. I couldn't have told on him anyway; I wouldn't have known what words to use, and he knew that. I was an inarticulate little boy who could barely read and write, how would I be able to argue against a man like him? That was why he could afford to sneer at me and goad me, virtually challenging me to do my worst and see where it got me. It was as one-sided a fight as any of the wrestling bouts he liked to challenge us to. He could crush me in any way he wanted.

Boys like us didn't even discuss amongst ourselves what was going on in our private lives, didn't share secrets or open our hearts to one another. There was no way I could have talked about such things to complete strangers, because the shame would have been overwhelming. Had we all realised that we weren't the only ones suffering, that he was doing the same things to any number of us, perhaps we would have found some courage by sticking together, but our confusion of embarrassment, fear and guilt meant we never did find out about each other and so Murphy was free to continue doing whatever he wanted, dividing and ruling us. It would be nearly half a century before some of us realised that we were not alone in those days, that many of the other boys in our dormitories had been suffering the same fate in silence. It wasn't something that small boys would talk about; we didn't even want to think about it, let alone put it into words. It was much too painful and embarrassing. Even fifty years later I found it almost impossible to admit that I had ever been penetrated by a grown man. It was far too humiliating to speak about.

At first Murphy must have hoped that he had given me a big enough fright by just threatening the bad boys' school, and that he wouldn't have to carry it out. So, not wanting to be seen to be climbing down himself, he sent Jocky to find me and try to do a bit of arbitrating between us.

'Uncle Dave wants me to tell you he won't send you away to approved school if you apologise to him,' Jocky told me when he found me. My brother was obviously bewildered as to why I was being so prickly and difficult with everyone, why I seemed to be deliberately getting myself into trouble all the time. He didn't appreciate being dragged into the situation at all, but he was willing to have a go at saving me from myself, which was no doubt how it seemed to him.

'I'm not apologising to him,' I spat back.

Jocky tried to make me see sense for a few minutes, just wanting to smooth everything over as quickly as possible so he could go back to his uncomplicated life. When he realised I wasn't going to change my mind he shrugged and wandered off, having done his brotherly duty. He knew me well enough to know that once I dug my heels in I could be as stubborn as everyone else in our family. He was pretty much the same way himself about some things. It was nothing to him if his foolish kid brother wasn't willing to help himself get out of trouble; he'd done his best but 'there was no talking to Tommy sometimes'. I wasn't Jocky's responsibility any more than he was mine.

I could have apologised that day and avoided the new horrors that lay in store for me, but by that stage I had made my stand and I also wanted to be away from St Margaret's and Murphy, whatever the cost, even if it meant having to go to an approved school. If I had apologised he would have won and he would have been able to go on abusing me just like before, until I found the courage to challenge him again, if I ever did.

I didn't know exactly what a bad boys' school would be like, although I had heard stories from other boys about punishments and iron discipline that sounded pretty scary, but I did know it would mean I would be away from Murphy's night-time prowling. I held my ground and refused to apologise. There was no way he could climb down from his threat without losing face, so he had no option but to go ahead with having me transferred.

He was so highly thought of by all the social workers I don't think he even had to ask for a second opinion on whether it was the best thing to do with me; if he said that approved school was where Tommy Wilson had to go then none of them were going to argue. No one would have dared to undermine his authority. He was the expert in what was good for 'his boys'. Within a week the paperwork had been done and I was down to the juvenile court for a hearing that lasted about two minutes. They stamped whatever needed to be stamped and I was out of St Margaret's and off to the Dale School the same day.

I was immediately relieved to be away from Murphy, but apprehensive about what might lie ahead of me. Had I made a mistake? Was the devil I knew better than the one I didn't? Or would it be a great adventure? I would soon find out.

Chapter Eight

I was coming up for twelve years old when I arrived at the doors of the Dale Approved School in Arbroath, which was a few miles further north up the coast from Kirkcaldy. It was nearly the end of September, a bleak time of year when the trees are losing their foliage and the cold winds from the North Sea are starting to whip up for the winter. All I could think was there seemed little chance of any Christmas cheer coming my way that year.

Christmas at St Margaret's was always a magical time. The staff would work really hard to make it special for the younger children, putting up posh decorations and lights everywhere. As you climbed the first step of the stairway to our dormitories there was a huge arch with a large bay window, like something from a church, and they would fill the bay with Christmas scenes like Santa on his sleigh, being pulled along by reindeer, and the Nativity, and all the things a small boy like me believed in. And there would be carols playing constantly in the background, getting everyone in the mood for the big day. There weren't that many presents but what there were we really appreciated because we weren't used to being given anything. The kitchen staff would lay on a Christmas dinner with a party afterwards and Murphy would always take us out for a Christmas treat like the Edinburgh Tattoo, or to a pantomime like *Jack and the Beanstalk*. Anyone in the outside world seeing him shepherding his group of kids around would have been left with an impression of a good man doing a good job. They would never have been able to imagine the things that I knew about him.

It didn't look to me as if anything very magical was going to happen in the Dale School. I had been sent with only the clothes I was standing up in and allowed to take no personal effects whatsoever. I was admitted into a dormitory with sixteen small metal beds which looked more like a hospital ward than a home, with waxed floors and high windows. The only decoration was one large, gloomy picture of Glamis castle. I had been stripped of all possible sources of comfort and individuality, turned into an anonymous number, just another young troublemaker who was going to need licking into shape.

Being sent to a place like Dale was a punishment and they intended me to know that from the first moment I arrived. The staff wanted to 'teach me a lesson' and 'take me down a peg or two'. That was how they dealt with difficult boys like me, beating the arrogance and the evil out of us. I wasn't even a teenager, so they must have hoped they could force me to change my attitude and mend my ways before the hormones kicked in and I really started to cause trouble. Some of them might even have believed that theirs was the right way to do it.

The building was on the outskirts of the town, sitting in its own grounds. It was smaller than St Margaret's, never having more than thirty inmates at any one time. There was no way of knowing, from looking at the outside, the terrible things that were going on inside at virtually every hour of the day.

Normally in a case like mine I should have been put on remand for two or three months first, but that never happened. I don't know if that was because Murphy's word was considered to be enough, or whether everyone wanted to get my case done and dusted in time for their Christmas break. Whatever the reasons, I was put on the fast track to a new sort of hell. Nobody in the court had asked me a single question and I had been given no chance to speak in my defence. I don't know if I would have found the words I would have needed to make any difference, but they obviously didn't think I was worth listening to. I had been branded a 'bad boy' and that was enough for them. I needed to be taught a lesson and the Dale School would be the place to do that for me.

Years later I got hold of the paperwork for that court appearance and found that one of the questions asked was, 'Has this child ever suffered from a psychiatric disorder?' The answer given was 'No.' No one thought to mention that I had been in a psychiatric unit at Ovenstone for a full year when I was five years old and had been on antidepressants ever since. I guess they thought that would confuse the picture, making me 'disturbed' rather than just plain 'bad', and a disturbed child might need a great deal more care and attention.

Even though I had heard the rumours whispered in the dormitories at St Margaret's about the levels of violence used to punish and discipline pupils, I had no real idea what a 'bad boy school' was until I actually walked through the gates at Dale. But within minutes I was left in no doubt that I had arrived in hell and there was going to be nobody there to save me.

Dale was run by a married couple, who both liked to show us inmates exactly who was the boss from the moment we arrived. The idea was to put us in our places and make us fear them. They were both tall, or seemed so to me. He was about six foot with a medium build. His hair was always brushed back and thick with Brylcreem, the smell reminding me of Murphy. Unlike Murphy he was a heavy chain-smoker and his clothes always stank of stale tobacco. His wife was only a few inches shorter than him and broadly built. She looked on herself as Madam Muck and we had to call her 'Ma'am', just like the Queen. He was about forty-two and she was a few years younger, but to me they seemed old and steeped in evil.

For the first few days at Dale my life was nothing but a series of unprovoked beatings from many of the staff, especially the McAllisters, to show me exactly what would happen if I ever stepped out of line for even a second while I was with them. Although the regime was the same for everyone when they first arrived, it seemed to me that I was more harshly treated than most. Maybe they thought I wasn't getting the message. Maybe Murphy had let it be known that I was a particularly difficult boy, a liar and a thief, and they were making sure I didn't think I would receive the same sort of leniency at Dale that they probably believed I had enjoyed at St Margaret's.

Physically I was still only a small boy and the force of their kicks, punches and slaps would knock me off my feet every time they landed. My back and my bottom were raw from the leather belts they used all the time on me, thrashing at the same time as they kicked and punched me in whichever direction they wanted me to go, whipping me like a dog. This, I have since discovered, was how the approved school system was run all over Britain in the sixties. At one time it was referred to by politicians as the 'short sharp shock treatment'. It is hard to imagine how it could ever achieve anything other than make boys angrier, more disturbed and more violent in the long run. I can't believe it is possible to beat anyone into being a 'good' person.

Murphy used to dole out physical punishment as well, but nothing on this scale. If two of us were messing about he would bang our heads together, and once or twice he threw me up against a wall with all his strength when he was angry with me, but it was never systematic beating like this. Sometimes Murphy would seem a bit sadistic, making out he was doing something for our own good, like taking us out onto the sea in a sailing boat and then chucking us over the side, even though he knew we couldn't swim. I can remember the terror of going under the freezing waves when he decided it was my turn, then finding I had bobbed back up, swallowing what felt like gallons of cold salty water, only to sink straight down again, thrashing wildly in my attempts to pull myself back to the surface. I thought I was going to die when I realised I was about to go down for the third time, but Murphy hauled me back into the boat at the last minute. Maybe he thought such shock tactics would teach me how to swim, but it didn't and it was a terrifying experience. He used to take us to the local swimming pool too and other boys later came forward to accuse him of abusing them in the changing rooms, but I don't remember him ever doing that to me.

Another boy later claimed that he had actually been sexually abused in the boat, bent over the side and buggered by Murphy when the two of them were out at sea on their own, but I don't remember that ever happening to me either. I do remember him once pushing my head down the toilet pan and then flushing it when he was angry with me about something. But nothing he had ever done was as constant and vicious and frightening as the Dale School regime. And now I didn't even have Jocky's comforting presence in the background to remind me that I did have a family, even if they didn't care about me, that I had come from somewhere and did once belong to someone. Now I was completely isolated and alone in a threatening, alien world.

Apart from being free of Murphy's night-time visits, the only other advantage for me of being in Dale was that they gave us a few weeks home leave at Easter and Christmas and in the summer. When I realised I would be going home for a visit in just three months it made me think I could survive. I just had to hold on and then I would be able to tell my mum how bad it was and she could do something about it. I don't know what made me think she would be any more interested than she had been about St Margaret's, but I must still have held some childish faith in her maternal instincts, despite everything she had done to prove she had none.

Because there were so few lads in the school, when the staff wanted a holiday themselves they simply closed the place down. I was told that if I was bad they would cancel my home leave and send me to another approved school for the holiday instead. They seemed to be angry with me all the time so it was hard to tell if I was being bad or not, but once I'd given up all hope of escaping I did my best to please them and to obey every order, clinging onto the hope of being home for Christmas.

I had been wondering what to get Mum as a Christmas present, to show her how much I loved her and how sorry I was for being so much trouble, when the perfect gift seemed to practically fall out of the sky at my feet. I was crossing the local golf course one Saturday afternoon on the way to watch a football match and found a silver Ronson lighter that one of the golfers must have dropped. Instead of handing it in, as I know I should have done, I decided to give it to Mum. It was the perfect present for someone who smoked as much as she did. When I got back to the school I crept into the cloakrooms, trying to look innocent. Climbing up onto the seat of one of the toilets I lifted the lid on the cistern and slid the lighter inside, thinking it would be safe there until it was time to go home, when I could retrieve it for her.

I guess it was an obvious hiding place that inmates had used before and the staff must have been checking the cisterns regularly. They found the lighter but said nothing, instead setting a trap with some red dye to catch whoever had put it there.

Then they waited patiently for their prey to return.

When I went to fetch it just before I was due to go home for Christmas, I was literally caught red-handed. I tried desperately to scrub the incriminating stain off my palms when I realised what had happened, but there was no way I could get rid of it and my crime cost me my Christmas with the family. I was sent instead to an establishment called Mossbank in Glasgow, which was a much bigger school than Dale, with around a hundred lads, ninety per cent of them older than me. Mossbank stayed open for business all the time. With each punishment I seemed to be getting further and further from home. Kirkcaldy now seemed a million miles away and I kept thinking of everything I was missing at St Margaret's as Christmas Day passed without any recognition from anyone.

The staff at Dale must have known that I had psychiatric problems just from observing my behaviour, even if Murphy hadn't passed on the report about my stay in Ovenstone. For a start I was still wetting the bed, even though I was now twelve years old. At St Margaret's they had been very understanding about it, just quietly taking the soiled bedclothes away to the laundry to be washed in the morning, never telling me off or beating me or humiliating me in front of the others. I guess they believed that if they treated me with kindness I would grow out of it quicker than if they made a big fuss about it. There had even been a time, when Murphy had left me alone for two or three months, that I stopped wetting the bed at all. As soon as he started using me again the problem began once more. Unsurprisingly, the beatings at Dale made me a hundred times worse.

At Dale they did not tolerate such aberrant behaviour and I had to be punished every time it happened. The more frightened I was of doing it, the more likely it was to happen. The moment they woke me in the morning they would check the sheets, so there was no chance I could do anything to try to hide what had happened. I would barely have time to gather my thoughts and work out what was going on before they dragged me from the bed, my soaked, stinking pyjamas sticking to my legs, humiliated in front of all the other boys. I would then be kicked and punched and pushed down the stairs and along the corridors, being battered all the way into the changing rooms where there were showers and baths and cold tiled floors. I would be stripped naked and plunged into a freezing bath. Then, shivering and shocked, I would be forced to scrub my soiled sheets with a bar of carbolic soap in the same icy water I had just washed myself in.

I'd try to stay awake as long as possible at night, for fear that I would do it again, giving myself as little time asleep as possible, believing that would lessen the chances that I would have an accident. But it didn't work, it just made me sleep even deeper when I did eventually have to give in to the tiredness, and left me exhausted during the day. I began to fall asleep in the classroom at school, which would anger the teachers and reinforce the idea that I was just a bad boy, a lad who wasn't worth helping because he didn't care about anything and wasn't even trying to better himself. The bed-wetting was always worse just after I came back from a home leave, when I was trying to adjust to being taken away from my family and to being beaten almost constantly.

There were other sins I was committing virtually every day, like not being able to do my shoelaces up. I never had been able to master bows and knots, however hard I tried, but it was a rule of the school that we all had to do our laces up smartly every morning, like soldiers going out on parade. The staff would become infuriated as they waited for me or saw me walking about with my laces trailing in the mud, and would batter me for being so backward. They would then force me to sit for hours until I had mastered the knots, and it did take hours; my fingers just didn't seem able to follow the instructions my brain was trying to give them. Even if I did master it, by the next day I would forget the sequence of movements and would have to go through the whole thing again. I could never remember which lace was supposed to go over which to create a firm knot, and the more they shouted at me and hit me the harder it was to think straight. The more I fumbled and failed the more I panicked and the clumsier I became.

Mrs McAllister was as violent as her husband, and in some ways it was more frightening to be beaten and punched and kicked by a woman than by a man. Even though I was used to Mum's temper tantrums I was still shivering and unnerved by the ferocity of this woman's attacks. Far too many of the staff at the Dale School behaved in a similar way; I guess they were told that if they didn't break our spirits and teach us our place quickly we would take liberties and they would never be able to keep control. Maybe they believed they were doing the right thing, teaching us to be better behaved and obedient, but I'm not sure they even thought about it that much. They had been given permission to beat us all they wanted and that was enough for them; some of them seemed to enjoy it.

The physical abuse was so bad a group of us decided to run away together, though we knew we would be punished with even more intense beatings if we were caught. It was a boy called Billy Sutherland who first hatched the idea, and we plotted and planned for three days before finally plucking up the courage to slip out down the fire escape during the night. We were all confident we would get away with it and that the authorities would never find us, although I don't know where we thought we could go or who could possibly help us, particularly after my experience of running away from St Margaret's. We slipped out of the grounds into the surrounding fields, munching on some of the farmer's turnips as we found our way to a main road. Within a few hours a police car cruised up and we were back in custody, and in big trouble. The one thing they had been trying to do was break our spirit and by running away we had shown them that they hadn't succeeded in their goal, that we still had some fight left in us. It was like we had challenged them to try harder, a challenge they were more than happy to rise to.

Believing they had to make an example of us to ensure no one else tried to emulate what we had done, they ordered us to the dormitories to change into thin gym shorts as soon as the police delivered us back, and then made us line up in single file. We knew exactly what that meant and we even put up a bit of a struggle, but it was hopeless. Three burly members of staff took us off one by one to the playroom, holding us each down in turn while another gave us such a hiding with a leather belt that we were red raw for weeks afterwards. The playroom was two floors down, so those of us who were waiting couldn't hear what was going on, but we could see the state of the other boys as they made their way back up past us to the dormitories with tear-stained faces and wobbling legs.

Eventually it was my turn. The blows just kept on coming like they would never end, and I had to struggle even to stay conscious against the pain. Our sad little bid for freedom had only proved one thing: that there was no escape for bad boys like us, not till we had served our time and learned our lesson. No one at Dale was going to be showing us any mercy. Many years later McAllister was charged for abuse and assault. He went on trial but the case was found 'not proven', due to lack of evidence. Even though he is now dead there is still another case in the Court of Sessions at Edinburgh against the managers of Dale School, waiting to be heard.

There was no one for us to go to for help. There was never any aftercare, and no social workers came to see us. The only person we were allowed to appeal to about anything was the head man himself, and he was the most violent of them all and would never have thought that we had a case for any sort of complaint. Alongside his wife he was as much of an all-powerful god at Dale as Murphy had been at St Margaret's. Sometimes I would try to get permission to go outside to play, or to knock about with some kids I might have befriended during the day at Arbroath Academy, the local school, but it was never granted. I was never trusted again after the first escape attempt.

Each day we would all go to the local school for lessons and I would try my best to keep up with the other children, even though I still couldn't really read or write properly. I understood that it was important to get as much education as possible if I ever wanted to have a better life than Dad and most of the other men I knew in Kirkcaldy, but by then I had fallen so far behind I needed remedial teaching, which I was never going to get. Nothing like that was on offer to inmates from Dale, they didn't seem to see it as something directly related to our behaviour or to our chances of making good in our adult lives. So I just had to keep struggling on, out of my depth as surely as when Murphy threw me into the sea, amongst kids from proper homes who had never had their schooling interrupted. It was like I was constantly sliding backwards in life when everyone else was moving forward, unable to get a grip on anything in order to better myself.

Whatever happened, even if they had brought in special needs teachers, I was never going to be academic; my interests lay more in sport and practical subjects like woodwork. By the time I left Arbroath Academy, however, I could at least read and write, so some good came of my time in that school. Every Sunday at Dale we were made to sit down to write letters to our mothers. To start with I had to ask someone else to do it for me, but once I'd mastered the writing part of it I found I actually enjoyed the weekly task. Each time I would start out my letter feeling warm and comfortable at the thought of talking to Mum on the page, where she couldn't interrupt me or ignore me or tell me to shut up. It felt like a chance to actually have her listen to me. I would start to pour my heart out and by the end I would be crying, realising all over again how much I was missing her and how miserable I was at Dale. The maternal bond must be incredibly strong for children, because no matter how often Mum hit me or shouted at me, let me down and disappointed me, I still wanted to be at home with her more than anywhere else.

On the few occasions when I was allowed to go home from Dale on leave I tried to explain to her what it was like there and how violent the staff were, but I could tell she wasn't interested. She didn't see it as her problem, and I suppose it wasn't really. I soon realised she was never going to do anything about it. What could she have done, anyway? They were hardly going to change the system because someone's mother had complained. It would have been nice to have thought she at least cared a bit about what was happening to me, but she was too busy worrying about where her next bingo money was coming from. I suppose there is a time in every boy's life when he realises he is on his own and that there is nothing his parents can or will do to help any more. It's surprising that I held out hope for as long as I did.

The rough treatment didn't end at Dale. While doing training at Polmont Borstal in Falkirk, my spirits sank so low I eventually could see no point in going on with the struggle to survive. We had to spend the first eight weeks of training in an Allocation Unit, which was like a prison camp with everything done at the double and no questions asked. The regime was just as cruel as Dale, and all I wanted was to end my life and stop the constant pain and unhappiness. If this was what my life was always going to be like I didn't want any more of it. One evening, alone in my cell, I decided to end it once and for all. I tied together a few bootlaces and made a noose, intending to hang myself from the bars of the window. I can't be sure now whether I expected it to work, or whether I was just trying to shock the authorities into realising what a bad state I was in. But I remember how terribly desperate and hopeless I felt.

Doing a spot check of the cells, a member of staff saw the makeshift gallows and set off the alarm. It seemed I had finally managed to catch their attention. They barged into my cell with a lot of shouting and panic and cut me free before I had a chance to really harm myself. They finally realised I was more disturbed than they had thought, or been led to believe by Murphy, and wanted to find out what was going on in my head to make me decide on such a drastic course. I was marched off to see the resident psychologist, who sat me down to talk in the hope of unravelling all the knots in my brain.

The poor man did his best to try to find out what it was that was causing my depression, like many others after him, but there was no way I was going to be able to talk to him or anyone else about Murphy and what had happened to me at St Margaret's. The years of physical abuse had forced me to block out the unwanted memories. The secrets of those nights with Murphy were locked safely away, and a few hours with a psychologist I didn't trust would not even touch on the damage inside my head.

All the psychologist saw sitting in front of him was a sullen, silent, unco-operative boy who had trouble communicating with anyone beyond shrugs and grunts. I dare say I seemed pretty typical to him of all the boys he had seen in Polmont. I couldn't tell him why I wanted to end my life because I didn't really know myself. I never thought about Murphy any more or the things he had done to me. It was the only way I could survive day to day. The only thing the doctors could think to do for me was increase my doses of antidepressants to try to keep me on an even keel.

It wasn't until I'd been at Dale for over a year that the staff started to go a bit easier on me; maybe I had finally realised I had to knuckle down and do what they said without question. Or maybe they actually had managed to break my spirit and their brutal system had had the desired effect from their point of view.

I don't know what happened to most of the other lads who were in Dale at the same time I was. I've never been a great one for keeping in contact with people once they are no longer part of my day-to-day life. I did, however, hear about one of the lads that I escaped with, Billy Sutherland, and I only know what happened because I read about him in the papers many years later. The story was he became a rent boy after he was released and was picked up by a man called Dennis Nielsen, a notorious serial killer of the time. Billy ended up being one of the fifteen known victims that Nielsen murdered and mutilated in his flat in London. It was a shockingly violent end to a young life (Billy was just twenty-seven when he was killed), but violence was all there was at Dale; it was what they taught us, all day and every day. It seems likely to me that most of the boys who end up selling their bodies on the streets would have been brutalised in one way or another as children, either in the care system or at home. I dare say the same applies to the girls.

In the end I spent twenty-seven months in Dale. When I came out I was sent home to Mum and her new husband, Anderson, to get on with family life as if nothing had happened. I was still only fourteen and had to go to school so I was enrolled at Balwearie Secondary School, where the headmaster described me as 'an unsmiling boy who has been given great encouragement by staff, but there has been no response', and 'extremely truculent this year, unwilling to accept any form of discipline. Appearance has degenerated and he is now often very dirty.'

If they did try to encourage me I wouldn't have known how to respond because it had been so long since I had had anything positive happen to me, and if my appearance was degenerating that would have been because I was back at home where nothing was ever washed or cleaned or mended. Even if I had wanted to take pride in my appearance it would have been virtually impossible when all around me was dirt and mess. Everyone in our family seemed to have other ways to pass their time than looking after themselves and their home, mostly drinking and getting into trouble. There was no real family life as others would know it and I was very wary of making friends, preferring my own company most of the time.

I tried my hardest to stay on the straight and narrow because the last thing I wanted was to find myself back in a place like Dale, but I had only been back home for two or three months before I was falling into my old bad habits again. The hidings Mum used to give me when the police brought me home terrified me and they did discourage me a little from breaking the law, for fear that the police would become involved and would provoke her fury. But a couple of weeks after each incident the fear would wear off and I would feel strangely compelled to steal again, any urges I had to behave and not draw attention to myself growing weaker and weaker the longer I was at home. It seemed like I was on some never-ending treadmill, unable to stop myself from almost deliberately sabotaging my chances of making anything of my life.

Chapter Nine

By the time I was fourteen and a half I was back in front of the Kirkcaldy Juvenile Court on a charge of theft by housebreaking. I made no attempt to deny what I had done, I think I may even have admitted to one or two other things that they didn't know about, and I was sent to another approved school called Oakbank in Aberdeen, even further north than the Dale School.

As I was driven away it seemed a frighteningly long way from Kirkcaldy, and from the family I had only just started to get to know again. I felt a terrible sense of dread at the thought of being thrown back into another brutal regime of beatings and ritual humiliations so far from home. In fact, I was no more cut off from my family than I had ever been, but at least at St Margaret's I had known I was only a bus ride away from them, even if I had only taken the ride once, and even though it had done me no good because they sent me straight back and punished me for daring to try to get home on my own. At Oakbank even that option would be closed because I would have no idea how to get back, assuming I did find the courage to run away. I felt completely isolated from any roots I might have believed I had in the world, utterly alone and unloved.

Oakbank was three times the size of Dale, with around thirty boys in each dormitory. What I wanted and needed was the security, love and support from my parents and family that most kids take for granted and don't have to ask for. Instead I was becoming more and more cut off from the people who knew me and amongst whom I should have belonged. I missed having Jocky's familiar face around, although I didn't tell anyone. I wouldn't even have told him if we'd been in touch. We didn't tell each other stuff like that and so I had no idea if he felt the same way about me or not. I suspected he didn't give me a second thought when I wasn't around. Much like the rest of the family.

Despite everything that was going on inside my head, I must have been appearing more confident on the outside as I grew older, because a report written at that time by one of the staff at Oakbank describes me as having 'a glib tongue and a persuasive manner that masked the real Tommy'. How could they have known who the real Tommy was? I didn't even know myself, and with every passing month I was building a thicker and thicker shell to hide in. A supervising officer wrote that he thought he had glimpsed the real me and that I was anxious to show myself 'in as favourable a light as possible'. He also wrote that he had no doubts about my feelings of insecurity.

It's strange to read how other people viewed me all those years ago. I dare say their impressions were accurate, I guess I was after a bit of limelight and attention and I certainly felt insecure. How can you ever hope to feel secure when you have never had a home that you haven't been rejected from? Neither of my parents wanted me around and even Murphy, who professed to care about me and want to be my substitute father, sent me away to approved school when I didn't play the game the way he wished. Fathers should offer their sons unconditional love and support, surely? I'm not saying they don't tell their sons when they have made mistakes, or dole out punishment when it's deserved, but it is done to help the boys learn how to grow up to be good and honest, not in order to dominate them and bend them to their father's will. My father had treated me with a gentle indifference, whereas Murphy, my substitute father, had done nothing but exploit my dependence upon him.

The staff at Oakbank still used the strap like everyone else who was put in charge of kids like us, but mostly they used it on our hands, not our bodies, and now I was older I was able to steel myself to hold my palms out and take the blows silently rather than having to be chased around and beaten on the backs of my legs like a coward. The system had finally taught me to be brave about taking my punishment, but I'm not sure if that is really much of an endorsement for it. It just goes to show that eventually you can beat anyone into making a show of submission. Ultimately how I appeared on the outside gave few clues as to what was going on inside my head as I became more and more depressed, certain that the whole world was against me.

The authorities at Oakbank were strict about enforcing rules, but they didn't seem to enjoy the violence in the same way as some of them had at Dale. Mostly we got punished for petty crimes like stealing from the gardens. We would sneak out in the night and go to the greenhouses to nick tomatoes, which tasted all the better for being forbidden fruit. To the outside world we might have looked like a hard bunch of young men, but in reality we were just lonely kids pinching fruit and veg because we were hungry; there was nothing grown-up about us at all.

If we were caught smoking we were given a different sort of punishment called 'three hours', which was noted down on our record cards. At the end of the week we had these cards taken off us and they totalled up the number of 'hours' we had been given. If we had more than twelve we were banned from going down to the town on a Saturday. Oakbank was altogether a fairer, more civilised and normal place than Dale from that point of view.

There was, however, a bit of bullying from the older boys, mostly the usual punching and kicking, and accusing people of being grasses, and inevitably I was one of the younger boys they tended to pick on. Unlike at home, here I spent most of my time hiding from them, trying not to draw attention to myself, living inside my own head. Some of the kids had been sent to Oakbank for criminal acts, but others were just there because they'd been skipping school and stupid things like that. They probably weren't as tough as they seemed to me at the time, but they were older and stronger and I didn't want to get on the wrong side of them if I could avoid it.

There was a strong culture of sexual activity amongst the boys that I hadn't come across at St Margaret's or Dale, with a lot of them exploring their puberty together, slipping in and out of one another's beds and indulging in mutual masturbation whenever they had the chance. It was done quite openly with no sense of shame or secrecy, as if it was the normal thing to do, just like dating girls on the outside and trying to get into bed with them.

At fourteen I was one of the youngest there, the majority being seventeen or eighteen, and the older boys habitually bribed us younger ones with cigarettes or quarter ounces of tobacco to allow them to have their way with us. If the bribery didn't work then they would fall back on threatening us with a beating or with being sent to Coventry and not spoken to.

If I was standing in a queue to get my dinner, for instance, older boys would be making suggestive comments, laughing with each other, touching my bottom and that kind of thing. They would make out they were just kidding around, like they would have done if they had been doing it with girls, but they were all getting aroused around one another and they were always looking for opportunities to relieve their frustration. Although I was uncomfortable at being treated like some sort of sex object by these almost grown-up young men, it still felt good to have the older boys talking to me and wanting to be my friend. I was just so desperate for any form of affection by this time. I remember mutually masturbating with a couple of them, and I remember a third who came into my bed, put his penis between my legs and ejaculated. But even these events did nothing to reawaken the memories of Murphy that my brain had so successfully suppressed.

At the time none of it seemed that big a deal to me. It seemed almost natural since there were no girls around and teenage boys are always brimming over with hormones. I didn't particularly want to do it with them, and I probably could have stopped it by informing the staff about what was going on, but that would have marked me out as a grass and for the rest of my time there I would have been ostracised and bullied, which would have been a much worse fate. Anyway, fondling another lad wasn't such a terrible thing compared with the beatings at Dale. They didn't want to hurt me, quite the opposite in fact, and it didn't seem such a high price to pay for a quiet life. Many years later it would take on a greater significance when lawyers started arguing over where my troubles all stemmed from and whose respon-sibility they were, but I never thought that the other boys at Oakbank did me any lasting harm.

Reports written about me at the time by the various adults who had charge over me were never good. One described me as 'a most emotionally regressed boy, disagreeable and querulous, incapable of establishing satisfactory interpersonal relationships, either with his peers or with adults'. Which seems a pretty long way of saying I was difficult to deal with, angry and aggressive. Another said I was strongly anti-authority and living in a dream world. I had been living in that dream world all my life and I don't know how I would have survived without it. Everyone has to have somewhere they can feel safe, and there was nowhere in the real world that I could do that for long. But if I shut out everyone and everything else, I could finally relax. I was always content when I could daydream, like the days at St Margaret's when I escaped to the beach, lost in my own world for hours.

After a few months I was released from Oakwood on licence – which is pretty much like being on probation – and I got my first job with a fish merchant. I had entered the grown-up world and I actually had a proper job, paying proper wages. I knew that the authorities were watching me and judging me, to see if I could be trusted to behave myself. It was like some sort of self-fulfilling prophecy as I succumbed to the need to stand out and found myself in trouble yet again. There was no excuse for it, and no logic as to why I did it. I didn't need the money because I had my wages, but I would still break in somewhere for a few extra pounds, or to nick some scrap metal I might be able to sell for cash. Maybe I needed the attention because I had never had any from my parents, or maybe I was subconsciously fulfilling Murphy's prediction that I would never be anything but bad. Whatever the reasons, within no more than a few months I was back inside another approved school.

I'm not saying that working with fish all day is the greatest job in the world, but it was a good start for someone like me and I could have turned it into something if I had had the will to do it. Most people don't feel the need to get into trouble the whole time when they have a bit of money in their pocket, so why did I? Most people would have learnt their lesson by then, so why couldn't I?

I was always a really rubbish petty criminal, not professional at all, much like my father had been in his youth. I never laid proper plans or researched the premises I was going to break into. So most of the times that I committed a crime I was caught, and once I'd been caught I never made any attempt to deny anything or find excuses, and I would confess to anything else that I might have been up to which they didn't yet know about. Sometimes I would end up with as many as a dozen different charges on one charge sheet. It was as if once I started talking about my crimes, I couldn't stop. I knew what I'd done was wrong and I wanted to pay the price for it as I went along. Anxious not to build up some sort of invisible debt to society, I was keen to purge my sense of guilt. I assume most people steal to survive or for financial gain, or to get their next fix of drugs, and although there were times when I did it for survival, there were many other times when I can only think that I was hoping to get caught, hoping to get some attention from the adult world even if it meant being locked up or beaten as a result. It wasn't how I wanted to be but I didn't seem to be able to change my habits.

When I turned eighteen I became an adult in the eyes of the law and could no longer be categorised as merely a 'bad boy'. From then on if I committed a crime I would be treated like any other habitual criminal. I now belonged to a new set of official statistics. The older you become, the less willing the authorities are to try to help you change your ways or to try to understand why you are the way you are. To them I was now just another criminal who needed to be kept away from society and punished for his crimes, but inside I felt like the same person as the little boy at St Margaret's. It didn't feel to me like little Tommy had ever grown up, but I couldn't let anyone else know that; couldn't show any weakness or try to make any excuses for the way I was. I had to pay the price for my behaviour just like everyone else. It was like when I faced the strap as a child, I felt I had to force myself to hold out my hands and take the blows like a man, and not to run away and cry like a coward.

There were moments when the authorities must have thought they were progressing with me. At one stage I was transferred to an open borstal called Noranside, which was like a massive great farm with jobs for the inmates to do on the land. I got on well there, enjoying the outdoor life and the chance to do hard physical labour that left me little time to brood and sent me into a deep, exhausted sleep as soon as my head hit the pillow at nights. We had cells about ten feet by ten feet there rather than dormitories. Each cell contained a metal-framed bed and a bedside cabinet.

When I was constantly either distracted or exhausted there was no opportunity for me to slip into my old ways and steal. Within a few months of being there I had worked my way up to getting a job as 'Tractor Boy', which was one of the best jobs in the place. It involved driving the tractor (obviously), feeding the cattle and ploughing the fields. I loved it. I wonder sometimes what sort of person I would have grown up to be if I had been born on a farm in the country rather than on a council estate. On a farm I would have had plenty of chances to escape into my own thoughts as I worked, and there would have been less opportunity or temptation to steal. I might even have drunk less if I'd had fewer spare hours to fill every day.

Although I was behaving myself, the Governor at Noranside wrote about me: 'Despite his lack of intelligence he has a surprisingly deep insight into his problems. I fear he is a born loser.' Sometimes that was exactly how it felt to me, like there was nothing I could do to break the cycle I was trapped in.

Every time I was sent to another institution I nearly always ended up talking to yet another counsellor or therapist, psychologist or psychiatrist, as both they and I tried to work out what was wrong with me and how I might be able to change my ways before it was too late and my entire life had been ruined by petty crime and disrupted by prison sentences. Little progress was ever made and the real truth of my situation never emerged. One consultant psychiatrist's report describes me as coming from an 'extremely unsettled background', which he believed had left me unable to establish relationships. I guess they, and probably I too, were laying all the blame at my parents' door at that stage. As far as the outside world could see, the staff at St Margaret's had been the best thing that could have happened to me, given the terrible start I'd had in life, and I had been seen to reject their help.

When there were two such obvious culprits as Mum and Dad, why would any of us need to look further to find something even more damaging in my past? Murphy, the man who did so much for the boys in his care, would never have been on anyone's suspect list as the potential source of the problem.

'As a boy, he feels insecure and full of worries,' the report went on. 'He worries about his family and himself, about his parents and about his siblings. Apparently the younger brother is currently in an approved school and, according to Thomas, has run away at least ten times in the last month. There would seem to be no doubt that when he is on his own the situation is aggravated, and this is probably why he finds the cells intolerable. It is his basic insecurity arising out of his background that makes him unable to tolerate criticism or correction. With his background it seems unlikely that this boy will benefit much from borstal training. What he really requires is a lengthy period of consistent handling where he can identify with one person and learn the criteria for acceptable adult behaviour.'

I had so nearly had exactly that: 'a period of

consistent handling where he can identify with one person'. Murphy could have been my hero and my father figure. The way he ran St Margaret's should have set me up for life, showing me how to work hard and play hard and try to excel at everything I did. He could have made me feel that I was someone who was worth taking time over, someone with some potential in life. I might then have been motivated to please him, to make him proud. But because this hero had such a terrible dark side, a side that used and abused me and made me realise that I actually meant nothing to him beyond being a piece of meat with which to satisfy his lusts, I had no anchor in my life. Murphy had convinced me that no one loved me then or could love me in the future, that I was a bad boy and a liar and would never amount to anything. From those lonely borstal cells it looked like I was going to fulfil his every prediction.

Chapter Ten

Every time I was released from prison I would go straight back to the doctor in search of some sort of cure for the pain that weighed so heavily on my heart. Usually the doctor, unable to come up with any answers, would then refer me to a psychiatrist and I would be put back onto antidepressants in an attempt to balance out the chemicals in my brain once more and make daily life bearable for me.

Finding good jobs was always hard, and keeping them even harder. Over the years I would have odd jobs like going off to clean factory windows or do security work, sometimes being away for two or three weeks at a time. I liked jobs where I could spend the days on my own just wandering around factories with my ladders and bucket, or with a torch if I was on the security team, but even those jobs didn't last long. I had no staying power at anything. It was like I couldn't be bothered with life, couldn't see any point in trying to improve myself because I never seemed to get anywhere.

Each time I was back at home the pattern of my behaviour would be exactly the same. I would tell myself I was determined to stay out of trouble. In the moments when I tasted freedom again I never wanted to go back inside. It felt so good to be able to walk out of a door whenever I chose, to eat when I was hungry, to be able to go into a pub and buy a drink, to be able to take a woman in my arms. It was the simple things that I always missed the most when they were taken away. Things would always go OK for a few weeks as I set about finding a job and enjoying my freedom, but then the memory of what it had felt like to be locked up would fade, especially once I'd had a few drinks, and the everyday difficulties of life would start to weigh me down and make me anxious. Maybe there was a part of me that wanted to get back into the protection of an institution, away from the anxieties of the outside world, even though so much of me was screaming at the very thought.

Although I had expressed a wish to sever all my connections with my family, it was never that easy once I was living back in Kirkcaldy. We existed in a relatively small, closed community so we were bound to bump into one another now and again in the course of a normal day. I didn't even really mean it when I said I wanted nothing to do with them; they were still the only family I had, I just wanted them to know how badly I thought they had let me down over the years. I suppose I hoped to shame them into loving me, but there was never any chance of that happening.

I would see my sisters from time to time in the local pubs and clubs, but not surprisingly they didn't want to have much to do with me. We might all have shared the same family background, and experienced the same lack of maternal care from Mum, but none of them had suffered from the same psychiatric problems as me. There was no point trying to explain to them how bad I felt about my life because they wouldn't have understood. Why should they? They had been through hard times as well and they were just having to get on with things as best they could. It seemed to me that in their eyes I was always seen as the black sheep and bad apple of the family. It felt as if I had let them all down with my behaviour.

I spoke very little to my mother once I was grown up and out of the home. Since the abuse I'd suffered at Murphy's hands was still so repressed in my memories, I held her responsible for most of the things that had gone wrong for me. I blamed her for the fact that I had been brought up by the council's children's homes, and consequently for the way the rest of my life had gone. In her defence she would have said she always punished me for doing wrong and it was true she gave me a good hiding whenever the police brought me home, but she would still hold her hand out for her share of anything I might have got away with, so she could take it down to the bingo with her that evening. Shoplifting was a normal part of her life; it was the culture she had brought us up in, part of our routine, just like the violence that she used against us so casually. Then there were all the times she had let me down and all the promises she had broken. I found it impossible to forgive her for that and thinking about it was liable to make me angry, so it was better just to keep away from her.

I didn't feel the same way about Dad and I stayed in touch with him to the end of his life, often popping in to visit him whenever I was in Kirkcaldy. That would make Mum upset. I suppose I forgave him partly because he was a man and I didn't think he had as much responsibility to love and cherish me as Mum had, but it was even more because of the times when he showed me mercy and kindness, like when he refused to beat me just because she told him to. I knew he had been through a lot with Mum himself, just like the rest of us, and that gave us an unspoken bond. In many ways my life wasn't turning out to be that different from his.

There was one night that Dad and I were out drinking together, when I was still in my early twenties. As we lurched out of the bar I decided to break into Goldbergs, a local department store, on the way home. My tongue loosened by the drink, I told Dad what I was thinking of doing and he said he wanted to come too. I liked the idea of us doing something together so even though I usually preferred to work alone, I said he could keep watch from inside the shop while I went exploring, which he agreed to do.

Probably one of the reasons I was always being caught in the act was that virtually all my crimes were committed when I was drunk and not exactly thinking straight, or even walking straight come to that. I dare say I triggered an alarm without even realising it as I crashed in through some side window I had managed to force open, because the police turned up almost immediately. Dad was struggling to climb back out of the window when they arrived, so they dragged him through and bundled him straight into the police van. I hid in a changing cubicle and they sent a police dog in to search me out. I could hear it passing back and forth outside the cubicle, failing to pick up my scent, and for a moment I thought I was going to get away with it. Then the policeman shone his torch onto the curtain and spotted my shadow. He yanked the curtain open.

'Right, Tom,' he said seeing my familiar face, 'the game's up.'

Next thing I knew I was in the van with Dad. I pleaded guilty and ended up getting an eight-month sentence for that hopeless little adventure, putting me straight back on the same old depressing treadmill. Dad pleaded not guilty and was released on bail, but then ended up being sentenced to eight months as well. We actually managed to share a cell for my last two months.

'Why does Tommy no longer come to see me?' Mum would ask Dad from time to time. It never occurred to her that it could possibly have had anything to do with the way she had always behaved towards me. Dad would try to talk me into going to visit her because he always wanted her to be happy, but I wasn't having any of it. My mind was made up there. Nothing she ever said or did made me think that there was any good in the woman. I didn't speak to her at all during the last three or four years of her life and I couldn't even bring myself to attend her funeral when she passed away. It would have been hypocritical for me to stand in a church or beside her grave and pretend that I cared about her, just because she'd died. I don't believe she ever cared about me, or any of us for that matter. Jocky was there at the funeral, and he paid for the expenses. He was a better son to her than she ever deserved.

Jocky had always been there for Mum, quietly slipping her money for the bingo and never complaining about it. When he was just eighteen he saved up fifty pounds from his wages as a commis chef and gave it to her to buy a washing machine, but she never did, she spent it all at the bingo. She never had a washing machine, but then she never did much washing anyway. Jocky didn't say anything about the money, just accepted that that was the way she was. I probably wouldn't have been able to resist challenging her about it but he was happy to let it go.

He got on pretty well with Dad most of the time too, although he always said he worried about Dad's drinking. I didn't mind slipping Dad a few bob or taking him out for a pint. We all spent way too much of our money on drink, so I couldn't blame Dad for that. Jocky had Dad to live with him from time to time, but it usually ended up with them arguing and Dad being chucked out.

Dad was always buying drinks on the tab at the

Lister, his local pub, where they knew him well enough to know that his disability money would be coming at the end of the month. Towards the end of his life it was always me going to visit him, never the other way round. When I moved to England he never came down to see me, but then his health wasn't good because of breathing difficulties and bronchitis from all the years of smoking. It just would have been nice to have thought he cared enough to make the effort, but in my heart I knew Murphy had been right all along, and in my head I kept hearing his voice telling me that Mum and Dad didn't love me, that he was the only one who cared.

Chapter Eleven

Jocky's experience of St Margaret's must have been very different to mine, and for him it provided the right sort of stable base from which to start his adult life. Apart from the one year when he returned home to Mum and Dad with me, he had stayed at St Margaret's from when he was six until he was eighteen. It was his home, even after he had left school. He was so comfortable there that once he was old enough to work he stayed on, just paying them something from his wages to cover his board and lodgings.

His first job was as a commis chef at the Smugglers Inn in Anstruther. He told me that despite his grand title his duties mainly consisted of peeling potatoes for £3.25 a week, although he did learn how to make a great rhubarb tart while he was there. I guess he must have realised he wasn't cut out for the catering industry quite quickly, because he left there after only a short while and got a job working a fin-chopping machine in a nearby fish factory, still going home to St Margaret's to sleep at night. He didn't finally leave the home until he decided that none of the jobs on offer to young men in Fife appealed to him and joined the army, happily moving from one institutional life to another, swapping the discipline and camaraderie of St Margaret's for that of the First Battalion of the Royal Scots.

For me, borstal seemed like part of the adult world too. There had been no school lessons while I was in there; being able to read and write was considered education enough for boys like us. The authorities seemed to have given up any hope by then of drawing out some hidden depths that might save us from following in the footsteps of earlier criminal classes. I'm sure there were some good people working in the system who truly hoped that they could help us in some way, but in their hearts they must have known that with every passing year the odds against being able to change us and find us a better path through life became longer. It must sometimes have taken almost saintly patience from the staff who had to deal with the anger and resentment and stubbornness of young men like me when all they wanted to do was help us. I no longer believed that anyone really wanted to help me; I distrusted their motives and I didn't believe their weasel words. I always thought they were just waiting for another excuse to give me a beating.

The people who were working with us must also have known that once we were released from their care we would be going straight back to mixing with the same people we had mixed with before, falling under the same influences and giving in to the same temptations. How was it possible for them to break the cycle that our lives had become? They could try beating the badness out of us, or they could try understanding what it was that drove us to be the way we were, but in the end nothing much changed with either approach.

Now that I was an adult the world expected me to

work and pay my way. I had to try to get a job as soon as I was released from borstal before I could claim any benefits, and cheap young labour can always find someone eager to exploit it. Each time I was released, the day after I would be down at the jobcentre to see what was on offer. As well as the job in the fish merchant's I spent brief periods working in a hotel, a bakery, a car accessories firm and even training as a bricklayer's labourer.

Not being qualified for anything, and having a history of being a bad boy, I had to take whatever I was offered – 'No experience required,' the ads would say, 'training will be given.' Employers were happy to take on teenagers like me because they could pay us rock-bottom wages, the sort of wages no adult would be able to support a family with, so it was relatively easy to move from job to job whenever I got bored. I enjoyed being a van boy when I was seventeen or eighteen, delivering bread to the shops, but it meant getting up at four every morning and I only managed to keep that up for about eighteen months.

Once we turned twenty-one, however, and were classed in the jobs market as men, the employers had to pay us full wages, which meant it was much harder to get a job if you hadn't built up a track record for sticking at any one thing. My track record looked very bad indeed by then.

Within six months of coming out of Noranside I was back in trouble and back in front of the Sheriff. It was always for the same sort of crime. I started out breaking into sheds and lock-ups looking for scrap metal I could sell, then I graduated to breaking into pubs or shops during the night, pinching the most stupid things just for the sake of it.

Quite a few times I was pulled in for offences like driving without a licence or without insurance. I was always careless about official things like that, partly because filling in forms and taking tests and all the rest is hard when you can hardly read or write and your whole life lacks any organisation, partly because I didn't want to have to deal with any type of authority if I could avoid it, and partly, if I'm honest, because I couldn't be bothered to do the right thing. Most young people have parents or other older relatives who help to guide them through such processes, explaining what to do and pointing out the mistakes they are making, but my family was not big on that sort of thing themselves. They would have thought it was my own business if I wanted to risk getting myself into trouble. The only unforgivable crime I could commit in Mum's eyes was getting caught. Dad wasn't interested one way or the other and I had a way of alienating every other adult who might have been willing to help, like probation officers or care workers.

So often my crimes were entirely pointless. There was one time when I borrowed my stepfather's car without asking and managed to crash it into someone else. The smash only did light damage to the two cars but, knowing I had no insurance, I immediately jumped out and legged it, leaving Andrew Anderson's damaged car in the middle of the road. I don't know how I thought I was going to get away with it, but then I never did think through the consequences of things until too late. I'd seen the car keys on the table in the house, saw there was no one around and listened to the voice in my head, which told me to take the opportunity while it was on offer. There was no sense or logic to anything I did, no plan or goal.

Not many of the lock-ups and business premises I broke into seemed to have alarms in those days so it wasn't hard to gain entry, I just had to smash a window and let myself in. Even so I was never very skilful at it, nearly always getting caught. I'd never heard of the sort of alarm that didn't go off on the premises, but alerted the nearest police station that something was happening. The first I knew about that was when I was rummaging around inside an office, taking my time, thinking I had all night, and suddenly realised the place was surrounded by police. They would tap on the window and invite me to step back outside for a chat.

My lifestyle wasn't that unusual in Kirkcaldy. None of the lads around the estate where we lived had any money or any prospects, so everyone was thieving, partly to get enough cash to survive and partly to pass the time. There's not a lot of excitement to be had from hanging around on the streets or sitting around in the pubs, particularly if you have no money in your pocket. It was never hard to find someone who wanted to do a job with you, although most of the time I preferred to work alone.

Stealing money from pubs was a pointless exercise as I would end up spending most of my ill-gotten gains over the bar the following night. It was like a stupid circle. I robbed them; they claimed insurance and I ended up spending the money with them again anyway.

I never broke into people's homes. I could all too easily imagine how much I would hate it if it happened to my mother or father, my granny, or anyone else I cared for. People around us had few enough possessions without having them nicked or damaged. If some old lady had saved up for months to buy herself a nice telly, I would have to have had a heart of stone to take it off her, however easy it might have been to do so.

The drug pushers have changed all that, by making their customers, the drug addicts, so desperate for money they are willing to do anything, hurt anyone, in order to get even a few pounds to buy what they need. I might have liked my drink a lot, but I wasn't so hooked on it that I had to do anything that seemed to me to be unkind. I'm not saying it's ever good to steal under any circumstances, but I still had moral boundaries that I would never have crossed.

In my sober moments I was always telling myself I was going to stop thieving, especially when I had just come out of borstal or prison and knew that I never wanted to go back. The voice of my conscience was always there, telling me I would be a fool to take any chances because I never managed to get away with anything. I knew if I broke the law I was bound to be caught and locked up again, but whenever I'd been in the pub, which was most nights, and stumbled out around midnight, fuelled with alcohol, the bad voice would be stronger. It would overrule the sensible one, belittling everything it had to say, telling me to go looking for money, to take a chance, to live life and not worry about the consequences. To show the world I didn't care what it did to me, that I was still going to be myself and do as I pleased.

Sometimes I would have more than enough money in my pocket for whatever I needed, and I hardly ever had any use for whatever it was I stole. I might, for instance, steal a bottle of cough medicine when I was perfectly healthy, so there was no sense in any of it. There must have been some other reason for it, some other driving force deep inside me which I was only able to sense through the bad voice, a reason like wanting some sort of revenge on the outside world maybe, a world that I felt had let me down so badly. But the only person I ever really hurt with anything I did was myself. It was just a different sort of self-harming. Instead of slashing at my wrists with a razor blade I seemed to be deliberately getting myself sent to the sorts of institutions I dreaded the most. Maybe I wanted people to look at me and question how I had become this way, wanting them to ask about Murphy and the care he took of me when I was still young and could have been influenced for the good.

Even the police who arrested me, who must have seen hundreds of petty criminals coming through their doors every year, used to be puzzled by the way I was acting.

'Tom, why are you still doing this?' one of them asked as he was locking me up yet again. 'You've got a full-time job with a wage, why are you doing it?'

I had no pat answer I could give him.

'I have a few drinks,' I muttered, 'and when I come

out of the pub I hear these voices telling me to do these things . . .'

It's no good telling people you hear voices. They just thought I was a nutter, as did the courts, and I suppose I can understand that. The judges sent me away every time I was caught doing anything, each one becoming increasingly exasperated that I didn't seem to be learning any lessons from my experiences, didn't seem to be making any effort to mend my ways. I kept asking for psychiatric reports in the hope that they would realise there was something wrong, that I wasn't just reoffending to annoy them, but none of the resulting reports ever explained anything because I still wasn't able to speak about what it was in my childhood that had happened to make me the way I was. Over the years my memories of Murphy's dark side had been suppressed and substituted with the belief that I was and always would be bad.

The first time I was sentenced to six months in a young offenders' institution I found it quite different to a borstal. There was much less emphasis on physical training. It was as if they still held out hope with borstal boys that they could somehow exercise the badness out of us, exhausting it, sweating it away. The young offenders' institution was run more like an adult prison, just banging people like me up to get us out of the way of society and hopefully to discourage us from misbehaving again. There was no longer any real attempt to save us from ourselves. I was moving further and further into the realm of lost causes, caught in a vicious circle.

Chapter Twelve

Two years after joining the army Jocky met a lass called Malvina, fell in love and got married. It wasn't the most romantic of first meetings because he'd been humping sacks of coal to make a few extra quid during a period of leave and made a delivery to Malvina's sister. He was covered in coal dust from head to foot when she first set eyes on him, but he still managed to charm her somehow.

Jocky was in love and just couldn't face being parted from Malvina for a moment longer than necessary, so he decided to leave the army. Once he was back in Civvy Street he had a number of jobs, including going down the pits for a spell and working at the lino factory, but, like me and most of the other young men we knew, he never lasted more than three or four months in any of them. Much of the time he was drawing the dole like the rest of us. He and Malvina had three kids, little John (named after Jocky), little Willie (named after Dad) and Anne-Marie.

Most nights Jocky would be in the pubs, like most of the men round our way, mainly at the Lister Bar, and it was there that he started to develop his passion for playing darts. The Lister was a long single-storey building. Inside it boasted a drum kit and a singalong platform, which was quite often occupied by Dad when he'd had a few too many. All the bar staff were women which gave the place a nice friendly atmosphere.

It was always dimly lit in the games room apart from the spotlights trained on the dartboard, like it was some sacred, hallowed site. Darts had always been a popular sport in pubs, but in the coming years it would grow to be the biggest sport in the country, even overtaking fishing in popularity. I would play with Jocky in the pub leagues but I was never up to his level. The sport only started to become really professional in 1966 when a man called Olly Croft came up with the idea of organising the darts world more along the lines of other sports. Six years later the British Darts Organisation (BDO) was founded and an inter-county championship was set up. It was a huge success and by the beginning of 1973 there were ten teams playing. Today the BDO is made up of sixty-four member counties and has sixty-nine associate countries worldwide. The organisation now has over a thousand officials and a calendar of more than eight hundred events a year.

When Jocky and I first started going to the Lister Bar we didn't bother so much with darts, preferring to play crib and dominoes, but one night Jocky was sitting in the games room when a team darts match against a rival pub was going on and someone shouted that they needed another player. Jocky was roped in and ended up being badly humiliated by the rival team. The experience had a big effect on him and he started to practise at home, vowing never to let such a thing happen to him again. Being on the dole he had plenty of time on his hands, and he spent five hours a day at the board for a week until he felt ready to go back and try again.

As he got better he would use his newfound skills to make a few pounds here and there, hustling other drinkers, challenging them to games and laying bets, making ten pence here and there, moving from pub to pub through the course of a night in the search for unsuspecting new opponents. A lot of amateur players would supplement their incomes that way in those days.

Jocky had a natural gift for the sport and he just kept getting better and better with every game he played. Before long he was playing for the Fife County side, which was one of the best in Scotland. Every time he played the crowd of onlookers would grow bigger because he was also a natural entertainer, able to get the audience laughing at the same time as impressing them with his skills, like a knife-thrower or juggler might in a vaudeville act. It wasn't just a game of darts to him; he was putting on a show, particularly when he'd had a few pints, and maybe a few vodka chasers too. He would even get on his knees to play sometimes, just to entertain the crowd.

The act was helped by the fact that he had a pretty comical look about him by then. Jocky had never been any good at brushing his teeth, even as a young lad, and during his twenties he developed a gum disease which led to all his teeth falling out. By the time he was twenty-eight every one of them had gone. Most people would have had dentures fitted but Jocky couldn't be doing with all that, he just accepted what had happened and got used to using his gums for everything. He could even chew steak with them, provided it was reasonably well cooked. His wide toothless grin would become part of his public personality, along with his small stature (not much over five foot), and his fast-increasing paunch.

Everyone in the darts world gets given nicknames sooner or later, and they are seldom flattering. In his time Jocky was known as 'The Wee Machine', 'The Kirkcaldy Killer', 'The Mighty Atom', 'Spike the Bulldog' (because of his cocky swagger when he was on stage), 'The Fife Flier' and, most frequently and most appropriately, 'Gumsy'.

As in most sports that require skill and practice, there were quite a few years of living hand to mouth, with Malvina going potato picking to give them some part-time income, before the really big breaks started to arrive and change Jocky's life. The rooms he played in were always hot, making him thirsty, and there was always a pint in his right hand and a fag in his left. Having had no money for so long Jocky was easily tempted whenever anyone offered him a free drink, and there were times when he would admit he lost games because he'd had a few too many and wasn't exactly seeing the board straight. People like to gossip and there were those who said the drinking was going to ruin his chances of getting to the top of the game, but it was all part of who he was and why he had been as successful as he had by then, and Jocky was always the first to admit when he had made a mistake and lost a game because of having imbibed too much beforehand. There was no posing or pretending to be anything he wasn't with Jocky, which was another reason everyone liked him and supported him.

For many years he was the best player in Scotland even before he started to become famous in England and then eventually all around the world. He won a lot of local tournaments and championships and gradually progressed up the leagues. By the late 1970s he was able to earn a good living from doing what he had previously been doing just for fun, and he could finally sign off the dole. The BDO started to organise bigger and bigger international tournaments, and the drink and tobacco companies realised there were sponsorship possibilities in the sport because most people played or watched matches in pubs. Darts had suddenly become big business and Jocky was one of the first stars in the sector.

In 1981 he became the first ever professional British champion and Seagram's 100 Pipers whisky signed up to be his sponsors in Scotland, even though they knew he was more of a lager and vodka man. Jocky, the media said, was the hottest property in darts. In 1982 he became the first Scot to win the Embassy World Professional Championship. My big brother was becoming someone important.

Now that he was a professional there was no getting away from the fact that he had to travel almost all the time, and Malvina wasn't able to go with him because of the kids, which made it hard for both of them. Despite that she was always very supportive of him. While he was away playing in one important tournament there was a flood in the council flat above theirs back in Kirkcaldy. The water poured through the ceiling, destroying everything, and Malvina and the kids had to be evacuated to stay with relatives. Everyone decided not to tell Jocky, in case it put him off his game, so for four days Malvina went back into the ruined flat each evening in order to be there when he phoned, so he wouldn't know anything about it until the competition was over.

When he did eventually find out Jocky was all set to have a go at the council, but then decided that he would use his prize money to start buying his own house instead and give up living in council property. He was the first one in our family to be able to do such a thing.

When Jocky set out on the professional darts circuit he owned virtually nothing. He would turn up at venues with no more than a small suitcase containing a clean shirt and a wash bag, and he would have to hope he could hustle a bit of money by playing darts in bars in the evenings to tide him over till he had some winnings to go home with. Even at that stage he could easily attract an audience with his antics, and as he became more of a celebrity he was soon able to attract bigger crowds, as well as the media, who always like to have a colourful character to write about. Sometimes, when he was at the top of his game, he would be playing in front of live audiences of up to three thousand people, and the television darts competitions could pull audiences of millions, particularly when he started to appear on a television game show called *Bullseye*.

Bullseye became an institution, hosted by club comedian Jim Bowen, and at its height it was drawing audiences of up to fifteen million. The idea of the game was that there were three pairs of contestants, each pair consisting of an amateur player and a non-player. There was money to be won from hitting the bullseye and from answering questions. Professionals like Jocky came on during the show to throw darts for money that would be given to charity. By the end of the show's first run there was a five-year waiting list just to sit in the audience.

Once he had appeared on prime-time television Jocky's career really took off and everyone wanted to hire him for exhibitions in order to watch him play live. For fifteen years darts became his whole life, taking him all over the world and allowing him to buy himself a nice bungalow, a car and even a fourteen-foot fishing boat. We were all so proud of him; encouraged to think that someone from our family could actually amount to something in the world outside Kirkcaldy. When he was the first Scotsman to win the World Championship and it was on television for the whole world to see, everyone in Kirkcaldy was celebrating. They had seen their local hero make good. Nowhere was the celebrating louder than in the local bars like the Lister where he first played and honed his skills. He was treated like royalty when he arrived home with the trophy. Like the rest of the family, I felt nothing but pride for my famous big brother.

Jocky wasn't the only one who had had some success in his love life. I was twenty years old and just out of borstal when I met Elizabeth, a local Kirkcaldy girl, and fell in love for the first time. I met her through a mate of mine, Davie, who was the leader of a local gang which Elizabeth was part of too. From the moment we set eyes on each other we spent every moment we could together. I would meet her after she finished work each evening at the British Wool factory. It felt good to be in a relationship and to have someone of my own to care for and to care about me. It was something I had never had before, always being in institutions, feeling rejected or used by everyone who came into my life. Even during the times I was at home I was one of many, never actually being special to anyone. Now I could be special to Elizabeth. At the time we met I was living with Mum and Anderson, and Elizabeth was with her parents. Wanting to be together, we rented a bedroom of our own from Mum.

But even being in love, and having yet another reason to stay out of prison, didn't keep me out of trouble. My depression never seemed to lift and like many others I would drink more than I should, which made me more easily led astray. I was arrested again soon after Elizabeth and I got together and I was put on remand, which worried me because I thought it might put Elizabeth off me. What girl wants to go out with someone who is always in trouble with the law? I also needed fifteen pounds to get out on bail and didn't have any money at all. I didn't like to ask Elizabeth to lend me money so early in our relationship, but she immediately offered.

Her family were quite well-to-do people who had never been in trouble with the law in their lives, so they weren't at all happy about her choice of a boyfriend, but I was touched that anyone would be willing to do something like that for me. Her dad had worked in a builder's yard for thirty years and had fought in the war before that. Her brothers had all gone into the army as well. I can see why a family like that would have been horrified that their daughter was mixed up with a lad like me. Elizabeth and Mum fell out while I was in jail on remand and she went back to her parents.

When I was released on bail I decided to slip down to England to my Uncle Ronnie's house in Doncaster to make a new start and Elizabeth agreed to come too. As long as I was in Kirkcaldy everyone knew where to find me, but once I was down in England I could vanish into the crowd and both my family and the police would leave me alone.

It was the first time either of us had been outside

Scotland and after a few weeks we both became home-sick for Kirkcaldy, with all its familiar faces and voices, and we decided to go back. Once we had decided we couldn't wait another day and, not having the money for a train ticket, I stole a car in Teesside to drive us north.

It looked like a decent car when I picked it, and it was only once we were on the road, heading back north, that I realised it was running low on oil. If I kept going I was going to burn the engine out and strand us in the middle of nowhere. The problem was how to find oil when it was already late at night and I had no money on me anyway. I managed to keep the engine going just long enough to find a little village garage, but it was locked up for the night. We pulled up on the forecourt and I climbed out of the car, trying to look casual. There was a gallon of oil standing temptingly in the window display. Glancing around and realising there was no one in sight, I heard a voice in my head telling me to put a brick through the window and grab the can. As usual in moments like that, it sounded like good advice and I did exactly what it told me.

Hurriedly filling the car up, the sound of the breaking glass still ringing in my ears, I jumped back behind the wheel and drove on at full speed. I guess it must have been the wrong kind of oil, because by the time we got to the motorway we were belching clouds of dense black smoke from the exhaust, drawing a lot of attention to ourselves and unable to get off onto the side roads again. Inevitably, as our smog settled on the motorway behind us, we soon heard the sound of a siren pursuing us and we were pulled over. As soon as they checked out the number plate they realised the car was stolen and we were both taken into custody by the English police.

I was sentenced to fifteen months that time. 'I'm sentencing you on your previous criminal record,' the judge told me. I thought fifteen months was a bit steep for just stealing a car, but I was used to judges giving me the maximum sentence they could for whatever crime I was in front of them for, in the hope of motivating me to change my way of life. On another occasion I received nine months just for shoplifting. It seemed like more evidence that life was against me, that I was never going to be able to stay on the straight and narrow for long and that it was all my own fault.

So, within a few weeks of our relationship starting I was back inside again, eventually serving ten months in Durham. I was terrified that I had ruined my chances of making the relationship with Elizabeth work. It's a lot to ask a young girl to stay faithful for nearly a year, but as the months went past she continued to stand by me, writing me letters and coming to see me, and my confidence grew. Maybe this time I really had found someone who would stand by me no matter what, someone who would love me unconditionally. I couldn't wait for the time to pass so we could be together again as a permanent couple. As usual I was completely certain I had learnt my lesson, determined I would never do anything to get me put back inside again; maybe with Elizabeth's support I would actually be able to do that and change my life for good. I felt there was hope at last.

When I had about six weeks to go till the end of my sentence I was transferred to Saughton prison in Edinburgh, which I was pleased about because it would make it easier for Elizabeth to visit me. But when I got there I discovered there were some charges outstanding against me in Scotland, which I now had to face.

I was sentenced to another sixteen months in prison. I was devastated. It had taken all my mental reserves to get through the previous sentence in England, and I had only been able to do that because I had been working towards a release date when I would be safely back with Elizabeth in Kirkcaldy. Now I realised I could be facing an even longer stretch in an even worse prison, with no break between the two sentences.

Overwhelmed by the enormity of what I was going to have to cope with, and seeing no end to the months that stretched ahead, I became awkward with the prison staff, refusing to co-operate with them. I refused to take an induction course for them to work out the most appropriate prison to send me to, so I auto-matically got sent to Peterhead, then thought of as the hardest prison in the country. By being difficult I had merely made things even worse for myself, and I could see my dream of returning home to my girlfriend and a normal life slipping away in front of my eyes.

The prospect of being in Peterhead was a scary one, but luckily for me my friend Nip was in there at the time and I knew he would look after me. Even though I was no stranger to institutional life, I was still only twenty years old and could have been in big trouble on my own. Young men like me were always in danger of getting raped in a place like that unless they were known to have connections.

There was a hard core of troublemakers in Peterhead, men who fought each other with knives just to keep their places in the pecking order, and they sometimes even attacked prison officers for no reason at all. I was careful to steer clear of them, keeping my eyes down and my thoughts to myself, concentrating on surviving one day at a time. Generally, however, I found that the prisoners there had more respect for one another than in other, more lenient prisons. I guess they are all in for the long haul and know they have to make the best of it. I eventually served a total of thirty-one months in Durham and Peterhead prisons, which nearly broke my spirit completely. But most of the others were in for stretches of ten or twenty years, so I was a lightweight by comparison.

It's a cliché, but a true one nevertheless, that prisons are like universities of crime. You can go in for some minor misdemeanour like breaking into a lock-up, and come out belonging to a gang that turns over banks, or knowing how to blow open a safe or hot-wire a car. Prisons are the perfect recruiting ground for anyone wanting to find new partners in crime. Often, when I was serving my times inside, other criminals far more experienced than me would try to get me involved in jobs they were planning to do when they got out. I never wanted anything to do with them because I was always telling myself I was going to try to go straight as soon as I was released, but that didn't stop them asking. Had they realised just how often I got caught and how readily I confessed to everything they probably wouldn't have been so keen, but it never pays to tell anyone too much about yourself when you're inside. Everyone is looking for information that they can use to their own advantage; you have to guard your privacy and keep your wits about you.

Most of the prison authorities I came across refused to believe in the use of tranquillisers for prisoners and every time I started a new sentence they would make it hard for me to get the antidepressants I'd been prescribed ever since I was a child. Even if I went in with notes from my doctors saying that I needed them, the prison officers would confiscate them as soon as I walked through the gates and I often wasn't able to get any more until my sentence was served.

To be honest it wasn't just me, they didn't believe in medication generally. If a prisoner got diarrhoea, for instance, he was simply put on a 'milk diet', which meant he was given a pint of milk in the morning and another at night and nothing else to eat or drink in between. So inmates tended not to report sick, which was maybe the result the authorities were after.

Often my solicitors and social workers would refer me for assessment by a psychiatrist when I was in danger of being put back inside, all of them fearful that I might not be able to cope with prison life due to the depression and anxiety that constantly seemed to weigh me down. But every time I found myself alone in a consulting room with someone who was willing to give me a sympathetic hearing I would be unable to find anything to talk to them about. The key to the mental box that held all my secrets remained hidden, no matter how carefully the professionals might probe for it.

Maybe they thought I was just trying it on, hoping to convince them that I was sick when I wasn't. Maybe they thought they could 'cure' me of depression with a harsh dose of reality. Maybe they just thought I was soft and needed toughening up. Maybe they simply didn't give a damn; I was, after all, one of thousands of prisoners and I wasn't being particularly co-operative. Whatever their reasons, I always had to struggle with uncontrollable crying fits for the first few weeks of every sentence and would end up being put in solitary confinement on suicide watch, which just made everything even more depressing. I would be left with nothing in my cell but a rubber mat to sit on, feeling like a caged animal with no hope of ever attaining anything more than a temporary illusion of freedom, because it never lasted more than a few months.

Most of the time we would only be allowed out of our cells for one or two hours a day, but when we were out I would find a corner of the exercise yard where I could separate myself off from the other prisoners, and then I would sit and stare up at the sun, just as I had as a small boy on the beach outside St Margaret's, going inside myself, cutting everything else out, my eyes glazed by the brightness of the light.

Although being in solitary was difficult, sharing cells with other men was also a struggle for me, making it harder to escape into my own silent, secret world when someone else was talking to me all the time. Some people seemed to be able to adapt to the routine of prison life the moment they walked through the doors, but I would always take three or four weeks to settle down, feeling as homesick and abandoned as I had when I was first sent back to St Margaret's. It didn't matter that I was now a grown-up, inside I still felt like the insecure little Tommy who used to snuggle up to Auntie Margaret for comfort.

I never made a great many friends inside, just one or two, and I hardly ever kept up with them once I came out. Mostly I would just keep my head down and get through the sentence as best I could. Going in and out of prison like that meant that I never really made friends for long on the outside either, gradually becoming more solitary and isolated as the years went by.

I became deeply depressed in Peterhead and wrote letters to my whole family telling them that I didn't want any of them to come and visit me; that I didn't want anything to do with any of them any more. I blamed them for the fact that I felt the way I did. By writing to tell them I wanted no contact with them, I felt that I was ending the agony of not knowing if they would come or not. If I had severed all links I could forget about them, which I felt would be less painful. I thought it was Mum's fault I had been taken into care most of my life. Mum had hardly ever come to visit me in prison anyway, so rejecting her was a pretty futile gesture, but it made me feel like I was taking a bit of control of my life and trying to mend my ways. She was always promising to come, just as she did when I was in the homes, but she hardly ever turned up. It was impossible to kid myself any more that she cared about what happened to me, and I could see that she never had. Murphy had always told me that my parents didn't love me, and nothing they did ever led me to think he might be wrong.

I felt the whole family had let me down in one way or another, that Elizabeth and I would be better off facing life on our own. I was so confused by the mixture of anger and resentment that was boiling inside me, and by my own inability to work out what was causing it, that I couldn't make any rational decisions. Not having any medication meant that there was nothing to dull the pain, or make me pause for thought before venting my anger on almost everyone from my past. Ironically, the one person from the past I didn't reject was Murphy, the one who had done the most damage. I didn't reject him because I had blocked all the bad memories of what he'd done, because if I'd had the weight of those memories on top of everything else, I would not have been able to survive.

Chapter Thirteen

Spending so much time alone with my own thoughts in solitary, I still kept coming back to the same questions about why I was the way I was. And every time my mind went there I still met nothing but brick walls, blocking my path to any hope of understanding myself. Even then, with all that time to think and remember, my mind still did not allow the memories of the abuse to rise to the surface. It was like it had never happened. I could feel there were gaps in my own knowledge of my past and I believed I wanted to know more about my childhood in order to fill them in. I spent so much time thinking, but I never found any solutions, I just spiralled into a darker and darker gloom.

Gradually I was coming to realise that my own brain had put something off limits. If I wanted to gain access to these hidden chambers of memory I needed to find someone else, an external witness to my childhood, who could tell me about the things I didn't remember. But who could I turn to?

It was no good talking to Mum or Dad about it, or any other relative who might have been around at the time I was small. None of them were interested in self-examination, they wouldn't have understood why I was asking the questions and I was sure they wouldn't have been able to come up with any sensible answers. I was certain Jocky wouldn't have anything to say on the subject. I was sure he wouldn't even know what I was talking about, because to me everything in his life always seemed so straightforward. The only person I could think of who might be able to shed some light on what might have happened to me in those early years was 'Uncle Dave' Murphy. He had been the one who had watched virtually every move I made as a small boy, and he'd held complete power over my life for the most crucial early years. He had been my parent substitute and he was the sort of man who had been trained to deal with exactly these sorts of questions. Maybe he would be able to fill the gaps in for me and help me understand why I was always in and out of prison, always deliberately sabotaging my chances of succeeding at anything.

Desperate for answers and remembering the times when he used to tell me that he wanted to 'be a father' to me, I sat down and wrote Murphy a letter while I was in Peterhead. He, I thought, was the one person who had known me better than any other at that age, and that knowledge made me feel comfortable, almost as if I belonged to someone. I had, after all, been one of 'his boys'. I asked the social services department of the prison to find his address for me and sent the letter off without knowing whether he would even bother to reply. Would he think that I had let him down by ending up in prison after all his efforts to make a decent man of me? Would he want to have anything to do with me? Would he have forgiven me for being so bad, and for refusing to apologise at the end of our time together?

Even at this point, while pouring my heart out to him on paper, I still didn't remember what he had done to me all those times in the dead of night. Even if I had remembered, Murphy had been able to convince me from a very early age that I would never be believed, and eventually I think I even managed to convince myself that none of the things he had done to me had actually happened, that they were lies I had made up. So I put them all to the back of my mind, locked the door on them and threw away the key. But even with them out of my conscious thoughts, the damage he had caused to my stability of mind would not heal. That could not be so easily packed away out of sight because the evidence kept re-emerging in my behaviour, like a murdered body rising back to the surface years after the killer thought his crime was safely buried for all time.

The letter went off and to my surprise Murphy replied almost by return of post. Seeing the envelope in my hand made me feel good for a moment because it meant that someone in the world thought I was worth writing to, that I at least deserved a respectful response. I opened it eagerly and read it slowly and carefully, wanting to understand exactly what he was saying, but his words reinforced all the things he had told me as a child. He reminded me that in my younger life I had been 'a bad lad', who needed 'a firm hand'. Nothing he wrote triggered any revelations or new understandings in me; they were just the platitudes you might have expected from an elderly schoolmaster who had seen a thousand young boys go through his school and treated them all with the same disdainful, even-handed patience, firmness and amused cynicism. He didn't shed any of the hoped-for light into the shadows of my depression. He didn't illuminate any clues that might have helped me to solve the mystery of what was going on in my head. I was a 'bad boy' and that was the end of the matter.

Having cut my family off I was now receiving no other letters or visits apart from Elizabeth's, and she couldn't afford to make the journey that often. I had isolated myself from the whole world and from everything and everyone associated with my childhood. Murphy was now my only tenuous link to my past and I couldn't quite bring myself to snap this final thread. I wrote back to him after receiving his letter, asking him if he would be kind enough to send me the local papers so I could find out a bit more about what was going on in the world I had been shut off from. He responded generously, saving the papers up and sending them to me in a bundle at the end of each month. It seemed like a kind-hearted thing to do because he didn't have to stay in touch at all. No one in my family would ever have gone to so much trouble for me, and would never have thought about how much pleasure such a regular contact with the outside world would bring to a man in prison. It seemed that he had been right all those years before when he had told me that he was the only one who cared for me, that my parents didn't love me. I felt a renewed surge of guilt that I had let him down so badly.

'Your birthday's coming up, Tommy,' he wrote in one of the letters he enclosed with the papers. 'What would you like as a present?'

It surprised me that he had remembered, and even more that he was offering to buy me a birthday present after so many years. When you are in prison and someone offers you a gift you don't say no, so I wrote back yet again asking for a new pair of trainers, something that would have been much more of a luxury in prison in the 1970s than it would be today. He duly bought them, parcelled them up and sent them in to me. No one had ever given me such a generous gift and I felt genuinely moved as I opened the parcel, reminded of the many Christmases I had spent at St Margaret's. His generosity seemed all the more surprising considering I hadn't seen him for over a decade, and we had parted on such bad terms.

'You'll be getting out soon, Tommy,' he wrote a few months later. 'I'd like you to come and visit me when you're released.'

In my letter back I promised I would do that. I don't know if I actually intended to or not. I'm not sure that I really gave it much thought. It was just nice to think that someone from my past wanted to see me. It may just have been that I didn't get round to it but I never did take up his invitation, and never wrote another letter to him after I finished that sentence either. Maybe I felt uneasy at the idea of allowing myself to be drawn back into his orbit of power. Who knows what would have happened if I had taken up that invitation? Would he have sucked me back into his web? Would I still have been of interest to him now that I was twenty years old? Many of the boys were eighteen by the time they left St Margaret's, so they would have been more like men than small boys while they were still under his influence. It's possible that he did keep up his relationships with some of 'his boys' once they were adults and had left St Margaret's, although no one has yet come forward to talk about that in any detail. I can understand their worries; if I was embarrassed about what he had done to me as a boy, I would have been a hundred times more embarrassed if it had gone on happening once I was a man, old enough to say no and to walk away.

Maybe if I had gone to see him when he invited me it would have jogged my memory sooner, or maybe it would have made my problems even worse. If he had actually made a pass at me as a grown-up, how would I have reacted? Would I still have been too much in awe of him to protest, or would I have turned on him and done something that would have put me in prison for a long time? Fortunately, I'll never know the answers to these questions. For once in my life I had made a lucky escape.

Although I longed to be free during the months

that I was in prison, once I did come out I was lost, floundering around unable to find any direction or anything solid to cling onto. Elizabeth and I got a council house of our own, but even that wasn't enough. I felt that the doctor who had said I needed to live in a controlled environment in order to try to stabilise my emotions was right and for a few months in 1983 I was admitted into Stratheden mental hospital. I had been living in institutions virtually all my life and coping with the stresses and strains, decisions and responsibilities of real life was more than I could cope with. Once I had been admitted to Stratheden it was up to the professionals to look after me and make all my decisions for me. It felt a little like coming home, returning to the warm safe comfort of Auntie Margaret's bed or to Anne, the nurse who had been kind to me at Ovenstone.

The best thing about being hospitalised was it stopped me drinking most of the time, although I did sneak out to the pub now and then when the urge to lift my spirits became too strong. I liked the hospital environment, feeling comfortable and protected, although I started to suspect that the staff were using me to help them pin down the more violent patients so they could stick needles in them. They were good to me, the staff, so I wanted to help them, but I didn't like the way they handled the more troubled people. There was one patient in particular who was always attacking them and they would need me to help them subdue him.

The one advantage of seeing so many experts over the years is that I can now look back at their records and see how I must have seemed to the eyes of the outside world. Not many people have that opportunity. One of the doctors who saw me around that time wrote that I was 'certainly an extremely damaged man who is immature and has poor impulse control. It also appears from his hospital records that no treatment he has received over the years has made very much difference to his tension, anxiety or unhappiness. He is continually looking for a magical cure, always inevitably to be disappointed.'

Isn't everyone looking for a magical cure for all the things that trouble them? We think we've found it when we marry someone, and then we probably think it again when we divorce them. It's the impulse that keeps us all buying lottery tickets each week. Our logic tells us the chances of winning are negligible, but our less logical side promises us that if we do win everything will be OK, all our problems will be over, as if by magic. It is in those moments of clarity, when we realise that we are fooling ourselves and that there are no magical cures, that despair can overcome us.

Chapter Fourteen

When I finally came out of Peterhead, Elizabeth was still waiting for me, which meant a lot. No one had ever cared enough about me to make that sort of sacrifice before. We were immediately back together as a couple, despite all the warnings Elizabeth received from her family that she should get rid of me because I was no good. Looking at my track record at the time, I should think I would have been telling her the same myself if I had been her father. The fact that she was willing to ignore all their warnings in order to be with me made me love her all the more. I was certain that I wanted to stay out of jail from then on, to be with her and to show her that she was right to ignore everyone's warnings and to stay with me.

We didn't get married until five years after first meeting, when Elizabeth discovered she was pregnant. I'd just burgled a local social club and got away with a couple of hundred quid, so we decided to spend that on the wedding. We could have spent a bit more on it than we eventually did, only Mum didn't have anything to wear so some of the money had to go on kitting her out if we wanted her to turn up. In those days I was still talking to her, just, but things like that added more and more to my resentment of her and the way in which she made no effort to contribute anything to any of her children's lives.

Elizabeth and I were both really excited at the thought of having a baby. I had dreams of all the things I would do for the child to make sure that it didn't end up with a life like mine. I wanted to ensure that it knew its parents were always there for it, and that we loved it and even if we didn't have much money we would always do our best for it. I would lie awake in bed at night imagining what it was going to feel like to hold my own son or daughter.

When Elizabeth lost that first baby in a miscarriage we were both heartbroken, but in a way the tragedy brought us even closer and made us certain that we wanted to create a family. We went on to have two children together: a girl, whom we named Kerry-Anne, and a boy, called Darren. I was so proud of them. I felt they were the only real achievements I had managed in my entire life, but looking after them added a whole new layer of pressure to both of us and to our relationship.

I knew I was not a good provider for the family. I still never held down a job for long, I drank whenever I could and never got my head organised enough to pay the bills on time. I kept committing the same pointless, minor crimes and sometimes I would go into prison leaving Elizabeth to cope on her own, owing eight or nine weeks rent to the council, not to mention outstanding electricity bills and the rest. Quite often I had the money to pay them off but just didn't think it was worth bothering if I was going to be inside again, so I would spend it down the pub instead. Despite my many shortcomings, I still believe that I gave Kerry-Anne and Darren a better start in life than

I had. I was quite strict when I was there, believing that if they had the fatherly love and attention that I had missed out on, they wouldn't be taken into care

When you're living at such a low level there doesn't seem much point in trying to avoid getting into trouble, because you have so little to lose. All I wanted to do was escape from reality as often as possible, away from the depression and the hopelessness; and drink was the best and quickest way to do that. I can understand why kids today who live on the rougher estates are so easily seduced into drugs. They provide an even faster and more exciting escape route from all your problems, although that route leads straight to an even grimmer kind of hell.

Like me, Elizabeth was frequenting pubs whenever we had any money in our pockets, but we were seldom going out together. She would meet up with her friends and I with mine, drifting into separate lives before we had even really noticed it was happening. I guess we were escaping from the reality of being married to each other as much as anything else, and hiding from the responsibility of looking after the children as we should. When we were together we were starting to argue about everything, both of us believing the other was to blame for the cracks that were appearing in our little family, cracks that widened with every argument and every disappointment and every resentment.

Elizabeth believed strongly that my problems would be lessened if I just stayed away from Dad and my brothers. It wouldn't have worried me if I'd seen less of them, I liked being left alone, always had done, but we all lived near to one another and we were bound to cross paths with them every time we stepped outside the front door. I wasn't about to start ignoring them or crossing the street to avoid them. I dare say her mum and dad were giving Elizabeth plenty of ideas as to why she would be better off without me, and by continually getting into trouble I kept on giving them more ammunition to fire at me.

In my lowest moments I couldn't disagree with her when she yelled at me for being useless. What use was I as a father and husband if I was always disappearing off to prison? After all the promises I had made to myself about how I would protect the kids, was I behaving any more responsibly towards them than my own dad had when Jocky and I were little?

Leaving two wee children behind every time I went away made the transition to prison routine even harder to bear. I knew I was letting the kids down and I still didn't understand why I kept doing it. The guilt and the shame kept on building inside me, making me keener to shake them off with drink, which in turn led me into more trouble; and so the cycle kept turning.

I told Elizabeth not to bring Kerry-Anne and Darren to see me in jail, asking her to tell them instead that I was away working or something. Small kids accept pretty much anything you tell them. I didn't want them to see their dad like that, but most of all I didn't want them to follow the same painful road I had stumbled along. Although I couldn't work out exactly what had gone wrong in my life, I wanted to do everything I could to keep them safe from ending up like me. But despite all my good intentions I would then let them down over and over again by doing something else stupid and having to go away for another stretch in prison, missing another few months of their young lives, adding to the pressure on Elizabeth, letting them all become strangers to me.

For the first few years Elizabeth wasn't a bad wife, only going out at the weekends with her group of friends. But gradually she started going out during the week as well. The marriage was becoming really rocky; she and I just didn't seem to be able to talk about anything without arguing and shouting and I hated to think that the kids were having to hear it, remembering how we all used to hate it when Mum and Dad fought. It became a regular pattern; we would fall out and split up and then get back together again a few days later, both determined to make a go of it, but neither of us really knowing how to do it. Every time I was sent away to prison things grew worse as the distance between us grew wider. I could imagine a little how my dad must have felt on the ships when he was afraid Mum was playing around behind his back, although I had no reason to suspect Elizabeth of doing anything like that. I was constantly worrying about the kids and whether they were being looked after OK, feeling guilty that I wasn't there to protect them as I should have been doing. I knew that it couldn't be good for them to have a father going in and out of prison all the time.

By the middle of the 1980s my marriage to Elizabeth was almost completely finished and I needed to put some space between us so we could work out what to do. Jocky had become World Darts Champion by then and needed help organising his schedule, so for about two years I worked for him as his driver. I missed the kids, but I knew it didn't help them to always be seeing Elizabeth and me fighting. I imagine they were so used to me being away by then that they probably hardly noticed how much time I was spending with Jocky anyway. It was a comfort to fall back into the oldest and longest-standing relationship of my life. Jocky never asked me any awkward questions, never criticised or made demands. He was still as easy to be with as he had been when I was six. I felt proud to be his brother because he was still my hero. I loved being part of his show and experiencing all the excitement of the exhibitions and tournaments. I always felt warm and pleased when people wanted to talk to me because I was Jocky's younger brother. It felt as if I was part of him.

Neither of us had ever got round to getting driving licences and he offered to pay to put me through the test and do it all properly. His life was becoming more orderly than the rest of us; he had joined the mainstream and with his help I thought I might be able to do the same, breaking the cycle of petty offending and pointless prison sentences. I passed the driving test first time, mainly because I had been driving illegally for so long, but it took a fair number of lessons to get rid of some of the bad driving habits I'd picked up over the years of teaching myself. Jocky was careful to make sure I did everything by the book, like getting proper insurance.

We would travel all over Britain together, to whatever exhibitions and tournaments were scheduled for him. Sometimes, if there were a few hours to spare, we would stop overnight in hotels to grab some sleep, but more often we would be driving down the motorways through the night from one booking to another, keeping the costs down and keeping the show on the road. It was a bit like being a roadie for a band on tour. Sometimes Jocky would have a booking in Aberdeen one night and Manchester the next so there was no alternative but to drive through the night, ending up breakfasting on fizzy drinks and hot dogs in some greasy but friendly roadside cafe. In fact, virtually all our meals tended to be fast food and snacks, giving us quick bursts of energy to face getting back on the road, but sapping our health and strength in the long term. It was hard work for both of us, but such good money that Jocky didn't want to turn down anything if he could avoid it, although he hated being away from Malvina and the kids for even one night. He never knew how long his luck would last and needed to make as much hay as possible while the sun was still shining on him. I was very pleased to be along for the ride.

It was good to be back together with Jocky after so many years. We still got on as peacefully as we had when we were small, just two brothers hanging out together, a couple with so much shared history they didn't need to talk about it. In all the hours we spent together in Jocky's Volvo we very seldom referred to our childhood or anything that might have happened to us then. Neither of us would ever have thought to raise the subject of Murphy because I had blocked all memory of the abuse and, as far as I know, Jocky had known nothing about what was going on in the secrecy of Murphy's room at night, and would have had little to say about the man all these years later.

Being a famous sportsman and television personality brought Jocky all sorts of interesting work offers. He even recorded a pop song with fellow darts star Bobby George, and the press flocked to the studio in Manchester to watch this historic recording. The song was called '180' – the golden figure for the maximum score on the board – and didn't exactly set the pop charts alight, but it did get a few crowd singalongs going at events where Jocky was playing.

Despite his relaxed nature, Jocky did get into trouble with the sport's governing body once or twice for 'bringing darts into disrepute'. His lapses always happened under the pressure of a big match, a bit like John McEnroe on the tennis court, and the reprimands were always about using bad language. He would try his best to modify his usual late-night pub behaviour for the family audiences who now watched darts on television and at the bigger venues, but from time to time the rough and ready Jocky would slip out when he lost his temper. In 1982 he was actually suspended for three months because of his language, which meant he missed the Unipart British Professional Championship, a major date in the darts calendar. But while it was on he was invited to Honolulu instead for another match with a prize of ten thousand pounds, so even when he was in trouble Jocky somehow managed to come out smelling of roses. While the tournament went ahead in the wind and the rain in England, he was sunning himself on a Hawaiian beach at someone else's expense.

Business was booming but neither of us had any business training, we were just two blokes from the pub, one of whom had got lucky, and once the big money came into the darts business it was followed by sharp businessmen who neither of us could ever have understood. I'm sure it happens in any industry where there is suddenly a lot of money at stake, but when Jocky was at the height of his career there was a dispute with a former manager, which cost Jocky close to a hundred thousand pounds. That was a lot of money in those days, even for a top darts player, and suddenly he was having to scramble around to find enough to pay his bills.

He could no longer hand out money without worrying and after two years of me working for him we fell out over what I reckoned he owed me. However much trouble he was in he was still better off than me, and our last argument was over an electricity bill and a couple of weeks' wages that I was convinced I was due. I knew money was tight before we parted because he had already sold the fishing boat that he had bought in Scotland some years before, sending me up to collect the money from the buyer, bringing it straight back in cash. From that time on his career seemed to grind to a halt. He had had great plans when he bought the boat and he had even talked about me joining the crew, although I had no experience of the sea.

It must have been a blow to him to see her go because I know how much he loved that boat. During the years when he was recognised wherever he went, he would use it as an escape, heading off with his rod and tackle, his lunch in a carrier bag, wearing a thick jumper, bobble hat and anorak, sailing out into the peace and quiet of the Firth of Forth, well away from all the pressures of being a celebrity.

Despite knowing all about his growing problems I still wanted him to pay me what I believed I was owed. In the heat of an argument I stupidly lost my temper and threatened to go to the *News of the World* with an exposé of the whole darts business if he didn't pay up. Jocky called my bluff. He told me to do whatever I wanted and I took him at his word, storming off to the newspaper with revelations of tax evasion, dodgy business dealings and players sleeping with different women in every town behind their wives' backs (not Jocky himself, he was never like that).

I went back to Elizabeth and she agreed to take me back to see if we could patch things up. It was great to be with my family again, but I felt a bit like a stranger in their midst, the same way I had felt with my brothers and sisters when I was sent home from St Margaret's for trial periods. They had their lives and their routines and I had to fit back into them, but I didn't agree with everything that Elizabeth was allowing the kids to do and I found it hard to keep my opinions to myself.

Within weeks it was obvious to both of us that the relationship wasn't going to be repairable. We had drifted too far apart and both of us were too set in our ways, too stubborn to change for the other, and we split up again. In a way it was a relief to be back on my own, living quietly with my own thoughts, but at the same time there was a terrible emptiness deep inside me, like someone had cut part of my heart out. When we admitted defeat and parted for the final time we'd been married for nine years, nearly a third of our young lives. I tried to make a go of it for the kids, but it was soon obvious it wasn't going to work for any of us and I applied for a council flat of my own.

To my surprise the paper ran the darts story, plastering it across the front page and then across a double page inside. In a way I was shocked to see my words out there; I had never imagined they would really use them. I had never made any sort of a splash in the world before and I think I expected the journalists to ignore me, assuming I was lying. To find that I had been taken seriously and that my words were now being read at breakfast tables all round the country as if they were gospel was an uncomfortable feeling. Unlike Jocky, I wasn't used to seeing my name and picture in print and it hardly seemed real. I felt like I had exposed myself even more than I had exposed the darts business and I was left with a sick feeling in the pit of my stomach. It felt almost like I had deliberately caused a fatal car crash with both our lives. It was a foolish, hot-headed thing to do and it destroyed my relationship with Jocky, the only person in my family I had ever really got on well with. But at the time, in my stubbornness, I was still convinced it was the right thing to do and that he had been in the wrong in the way he had treated me.

My revelations must have embarrassed him badly in the industry. To have his brother do such a thing, to expose and gossip about all his friends and business colleagues for the whole world to read about must have been terrible for him. At that time his reputation was beginning to slip anyway; new players were coming up to prominence and his management didn't seem to be able to get his career going again. So he probably couldn't easily have afforded to pay me even if he'd wanted to, but at the time it seemed like a point of principle and I was tired of always being the loser in life. Knowing he had a brother who had insulted and accused of wrongdoing so many people in the business must have made people even less inclined to hire Jocky when there were so many other up-and-coming players.

I had never been jealous of the things Jocky had had in life because it would have been impossible to feel like that with someone so unpretentious and easy-going. I was just angry with the whole world and this seemed like one more kick in the guts for someone whose life had already been brought low. I had responded just like I used to when I was a small kid in the playground, rushing out and picking a fight before I had had time to think of the consequences.

There were already rumours of match-fixing going round and the professional darts business went a bit quiet generally for a couple of years after that. I heard that Jocky was having more and more trouble earning enough to keep up the lifestyle he and Malvina had grown used to during the boom years.

We have never spoken since I betrayed him to the press, but I know he is once again living in a council house in Kirkcaldy and that he has put the whole professional darts business behind him. I know organisers have asked him to come back several times, to make guest appearances, but I'm told he doesn't want to do it any more. He had fifteen years at the top of the sport, travelling twice round the world, and I guess he's satisfied with that. He always was such good company, content with whatever hand life dealt him. Maybe that was part of the secret of his popularity. He's an easy man to be with and I envy him that skill. Of all the members of my family he's the one I spent the most time with as a child, even though we weren't that close. I'd like to think that we will make up again while we are still around to do so, but I'm afraid we may both be too stubborn for it to actually happen.

In need of an income, I invested in a pickup truck and travelled around the local area doing odd jobs, collecting pallets and repairing them, selling logs as firewood, anything to make some money to pay the bills that were mounting up. I was so lonely without the kids but I knew there was now no chance of repairing my marriage.

Chapter Fifteen

My most recent prison psychiatrist had agreed with Elizabeth and suggested to me that part of my problem was my family. He advised that I would benefit from cutting all ties with them in order to break free of their influence once and for all. He suggested I should start a new life of my own, away from my parents and from all the chaos that surrounded them. In theory I had no problem with that. I had, after all, told them many times that I wanted no more to do with them, but every time I came back to Kirkcaldy it was inevitable that I would see them, especially my father and brothers, if only in the pubs.

It seemed like a good idea if I left the neighbourhood, but I didn't know where to go. I asked everyone I knew for some contact outside the area and a friend offered me a job working as a security guard in his scrapyard in Ashington. He would pay me a tenner a day in cash and give me a roof over my head.

The 'roof' turned out to be a broken-down old caravan which was parked in the yard and went with the job, although it looked more like part of the scrap than the staff accommodation. The site was a bleak, deserted place where it was unlikely anyone would be able to find me, or would even want to go looking. As I disappeared through the gates, which were kept locked, into this hideaway I was determined to keep myself to myself for a while.

It wasn't difficult to become invisible. The yard was hardly a place anyone would want to visit unless they had business there. The only people I was likely to have to see would be thieves breaking in to nick bits of scrap, and they were going to be as keen to avoid me as I was to avoid them. It was the middle of winter and the caravan had only a portable gas fire to ward off the chill, and gaslights which provided some sort of illumination in the gloom of the long evenings. There was no running water, just a standpipe in the yard that I could use to fill containers, and a portable toilet, which I had to empty when necessary. It was grim but at least I was safe and could be alone with my thoughts; no one to interfere with me or tell me what to do with the endless hours.

Living there I could spend as many hours a day as I liked lost in my own thoughts, just staring out through the caravan window at the mountains of junk outside, wrapped in as many layers of clothes as possible to try to keep out the cold. It was like the perfect metaphor for my whole life, to end up discarded in a junkyard, a grown man who was only worth ten pounds a day of anyone's money. It seemed to me that it had always been that way from the moment I was removed from my family at ten months old, not wanted or needed at home, dumped onto the junk heap of life. I was feeling desperately sorry for myself and had no idea what to do to climb out of the pit I had fallen into.

But even I couldn't stomach the solitary life for ever. There may be some people, the ones who become tramps and hermits, who truly can withdraw from all human contact, but I couldn't do that. Being left alone in the stillness and silence of that yard for twenty-four hours a day was too much even for my tastes. I knew I had to have some company or I would lose my mind completely, and the depression would take such a hold of me that there was a risk they would eventually find me dead and stiff with the cold in that caravan after another overdose.

During the separation from Elizabeth I'd met a girl called Sandra and we'd started a relationship up whilst I was still living in Kirkcaldy. We had been getting on well when I had to leave the area and I found myself thinking about her more and more, wanting to see her again. Deciding that I couldn't be alone for another moment, I rang and asked her to come down to the caravan to join me. I don't know what I would have done if she had said no, but she didn't. She actually seemed quite keen and arrived the next day. It was great of her to do that because my living accommodation was hardly the Ritz hotel and most girls would have turned their noses up at it.

Maybe she enjoyed the adventure of it for a while. It was different, after all.

We lived together in that caravan for a few weeks, like some sort of low-rent Bonnie and Clyde hiding out from the law, but then Sandra became ill. A freezing cold caravan with no running water is hardly the place to nurse someone and so she travelled back to Scotland to recuperate with her family.

If the yard had seemed quiet before she came, it was a hundred times worse after she had gone, leaving me alone again with only the rats for company. In the long silent hours my depression became so overwhelming there was no chance that even the most powerful medication could hold it at bay. I held on, sunk deep in despair, just existing from hour to hour, but after two or three weeks I couldn't bear it a moment longer and followed her back to Kirkcaldy. I knew she had recovered from her illness and I wanted to know why she wasn't coming back to me when I needed her so badly. It seemed worth taking the risk of coming out of hiding, because things back home couldn't have been any worse than the way I was living in the caravan. It was like I had voluntarily put myself into my own kind of solitary confinement.

I wanted to persuade Sandra to come back to me, feeling she was deserting me just when I needed her the most. I was having trouble thinking straight, feeling that the whole world was against me again. I was simmering on the verge of losing my temper as I travelled north, so it wasn't a good time to go and see her, but I did anyway. We met in the pub, as I didn't want to get involved with any of her family, plus I needed a few drinks to cheer myself up a bit. Not surprisingly we rowed as the drink started to take effect and the last shreds of my self-control deserted me. The aggression escalated and the row began to become physical as we both tried to force our points of view across, neither of us willing to listen to the arguments of the other. Finally losing the last of her cool, Sandra smashed a glass hard into my face. My temper exploded and I gave her a slap back in retaliation before I had time to stop myself, all executed in full view of the rest of the pub.

I was too wound up with the fight to know what was going on around us but the publican must have called the police, wanting to get us off the premises before we wrecked the place, and I ended up getting arrested yet again and charged with common assault and a breach of the peace. I'd only just arrived back in Kirkcaldy that day and already I was back in the police cells, after the bleeding had been stemmed from my cuts. Once they started to look through my background the police discovered charges I was still up for, and a few weeks later I found myself back in Saughton jail.

Despite our fights, there was still a strong feeling between Sandra and me. She took pity on me and was supportive whilst I was in prison, which I really appreciated. My divorce from Elizabeth had come through and I was feeling like there was no reason to go on, no reason to get through each day. Sandra's loyalty to me, despite everything I had put her through, touched me and when she came to visit me in jail I asked her to marry me. I genuinely believed that having her waiting for me would give me a reason to survive and to go straight once I was out. She agreed and we married while I was still in Saughton, and she moved into the council house I was then renting in Kirkcaldy. Because I was in jail there was no chance for us to consummate the marriage, but I felt happy to think that when I came out my new wife would be waiting for me, giving me a reason to want to survive each day At least, I hoped she would be waiting for me. Just like Dad on the ships all those years ago, I couldn't help but imagine what might be going on outside the prison walls as I lay in my cell with my mind churning. Would other men try to take her from me? Would she be willing to wait for me when the weeks turned into months? The days dragged by so slowly as these ideas taunted me, it was agony.

Then a few weeks later I started to hear rumours coming in from the outside, whispers and gossip accompanied by the odd snigger or sympathetic glance. Sandra was acting strangely when she visited, like she was being evasive. A few people told me that they'd heard she had gone off with Andrew Anderson, one of my half-brothers. It was news I couldn't dare to believe at first, afraid I might not be able to bear it. The feelings I went through, trapped inside the prison and unable to find out what was happening, or to do anything about it, must have been similar to the ones Dad suffered when he first heard that Mum had gone off with Anderson while he was inside. Was I going to end up like Dad? Was I going to be pushed out and forced to watch my wife live with someone else — my half-brother, of all people? The thought was so terrible I had to force myself not to believe it.

Part of the time I could cling to the hope that it was just a rumour and there was no truth in it. People in prison are always hearing things from the outside, stories that become exaggerated and distorted in the telling, driving them mad with worry or jealousy or a feeling of pure helplessness. I wanted Sandra to come in to visit, or to write and tell me that everything was all right and that she was waiting for me just as Elizabeth had all those years before. But no letters arrived and every visiting time passed without my name being called, leaving me with another night of anxiety and wild imaginings.

Eventually, after I had endured the agony of not knowing the truth for several weeks, Mum came to visit me. Seeing her there was a shock. After all the times I'd told her I didn't want anything to do with her, and all the times before that when she had let me down, I couldn't think why she had suddenly decided to turn up. Any pleasure I might have got from receiving a visit was ended when she told me the rumours were true. Sandra had gone off with Andrew and they were living together as man and wife in my house.

I felt like an outsider in my own family, just as I had when I was sent home from St Margaret's for those trial periods. I could imagine them all mocking me, rooting for Andrew and Sandra, happy for them that they were together and glad for her that she was shot of me. This was just one more sign that my family cared nothing for me, that I wasn't really part of their lives at all.

Once my suspicions were aroused and I started to question her more closely I realised Mum had known about it for weeks, but had only just decided to come in to break the news to me. From the way she was talking I suspected she had been encouraging them, choosing Andrew over me, wanting him to be the one who won the girl. It didn't seem right that it had taken this long for her to come and see me. She should have been the first to tell me, making sure I got the facts before the rumours came to my ears. She should have been watching out for me, doing the right thing. She should have cared about my feelings. But why would I expect that after all the times she had let me down and showed me she didn't care? Murphy might have had his own agenda for saying it, but he had been right when he told me that my mum didn't love me.

Unable to trust myself not to lose my temper and do something that would result in my sentence being extended, I stood up and ended the visit immediately, telling Mum to go and that I never wanted to see her again. I'd said it so many times the words were meaningless really, but they made me feel better. I was angry and hurt and sad all at the same time. I had thought I had a wife and someone to come home to once my sentence was finished and now I was discarded and alone again, betrayed by my wife and my half-brother. It felt like the whole family were laughing at me. Once I had got over my initial anger I wasn't that surprised. Mum would always have sided with Andrew and not me. He had always been a bit of a mammy's boy.

There was nothing for it but to end the marriage. It would never work now that I had lost all trust in Sandra and knew how much hurt she was capable of inflicting on me. It seemed to me she was no better than Mum and I didn't want to end up like Dad. It was easy to get an annulment since the marriage hadn't been consummated, but once it was all over I was left feeling desolate and alone. The hope that had been keeping me going had been extinguished and I felt I was back to fighting the whole world on my own again. Life didn't seem worth the struggle. This time my depression very nearly destroyed me for ever.

Despite the watchfulness of the prison authorities I still managed to make a suicide attempt. The weight of my misery became too heavy to bear any longer. There just didn't seem to be any way I could keep going to the end of the sentence: it seemed to stretch forward into infinity whenever I thought about it.

Believing I was always going to be alone, that I was never going to be of any use to anyone, and that no one else cared, I managed to get hold of a razor blade, snapped it into small pieces, wrapped the shards in lumps of bread and swallowed them. I suppose it must have been a 'cry for help' as much as a genuine attempt, because I rang the bell in the cell a few minutes later and told the guards what I had done. They rushed me off to the doctor but there was nothing he could do except keep an eye on me, feed me cotton wool which they hoped would pad out the sharp edges, and wait for the shards to work their way through my system, which they did, apparently without doing any damage on their journey.

As soon as I was discharged from the hospital I was back in solitary confinement and back on suicide watch with other people's eyes following me every hour of the day and night, just like Murphy used to watch over me all the time when I was little, always there when I did something wrong, always seeing everything. All the prison officers were interested in was making sure I couldn't kill myself; they had no interest in finding out why I was doing such desperate things, or what demons were driving me to despair.

I had made similar attempts to end it while on the outside a number of times, using sleeping pills such as

Mogadon, wanting to just slip away and never wake up. But I never took quite enough to finish myself off properly and always woke up again eventually, forced to face the future along with everyone else. In my lowest moments I was convinced everyone in the world hated me; that I was an outcast from society, just an object, like a football that everyone could kick around when they felt like it. If not even my own mother could love me, what sort of a monster must I be?

Although it wouldn't be quite true to say I never spoke to Mum again after realising she had betrayed me, because I would nod and say hello if I saw her around Kirkcaldy when I was out of prison, it would certainly be fair to say I never had another conversation with her after that.

Knowing that Sandra and Andrew were living together in my house made me feel even angrier, like they had no respect for my feelings at all. Every day that I was trapped inside Saughton and unable to do anything about sorting out my life, the anger was building inside me, threatening to explode. When I was finally given bail I stormed straight back to

Kirkcaldy to confront them. I had no plan of what I would do once I saw them, I just knew I had to go there.

Sandra answered the door, which was probably just as well because if I had found Andrew there while I was in such a fury, I might have done some serious damage and ended straight back in prison. Funnily enough, despite being really angry with Andrew, I still quite liked him. He had always been a pretty reasonable bloke, but the fact that they were living in my house was an insult too many.

Unable to take out my anger on Andrew, I turned on Sandra instead. She held her ground ferociously, as she always did. She obviously wasn't afraid of me and gave as good as she got, telling me exactly what she thought of me and why I was a bad husband. In the heat of the row I ended up slapping her, which I shouldn't have done and which resulted in the police being called and me being charged with common assault yet again. That was the end of my bail and I was taken back inside.

Once I had accepted that the marriage was all over I calmed down and finished my sentence. I then took the legal route to get the pair of them thrown out and took my house back. It was a matter of pride as much as anything else because I soon realised I didn't want to stay in the Kirkcaldy area any longer, living alone in a house I had imagined sharing with Sandra, surrounded by all the painful memories.

In an attempt to make yet another new start I gave up the house and returned to Ashington, since that was the only other place I really knew, and I applied for a council flat there. If you weren't fussy where you were you could get a flat in the area within six weeks at that time. Having lived most of my life in jail, and spent time camping out in a cold caravan, I was happy with whatever they came up with and so I accepted a flat on the Woodgate Estate, which was very run-down even then.

So, there I was, on my own once again, trying to work out what had gone wrong with my life and why everything I tried to do ended in failure. Things, however, were about to take some dramatic turns for the better.

Chapter Sixteen

With nothing else to fill the long evenings, and no way to escape the cloud of depression which constantly threatened to engulf me, I was drinking a lot in the local pubs in Ashington, and the aggression the alcohol would release in me would sometimes lead me into fights by closing time. All the anger and frustration at the way my life seemed to be going was constantly bubbling below the surface, and it didn't take much for it to erupt once the drink had lowered my powers of self-control.

It's never hard to pick a fight in a pub around closing time; there are always plenty of men who are up for it. I would try to make myself walk away from trouble whenever I could, but sometimes you have to stand up for yourself in those sorts of situations or you just end up being beaten to a pulp. Fighting had always been strictly forbidden at St Margaret's by Murphy, unless it was in the wrestling or boxing rings, so I knew it was better to avoid it if I could. I had got into trouble for fighting at school almost as often as I got into trouble for stealing, so I should have known better, but drink makes you forget what you should and shouldn't do sometimes and I had as much of a temper on me as the next man. It had got me into trouble on more than one occasion, and one fight in the past almost got me killed.

It began with a confrontation that started up as I was walking home from a bar in Kirkcaldy. It got out of hand and I ended up fighting out in the street with another man. We were at the back of a burger van and the fight was over something so stupid, like an imagined insult maybe, that I can't even remember what triggered it. I doubt if I would have been able to remember the morning after it happened, let alone twenty or more years later. As we slugged it out amidst the aroma of frying onions, dragging our tired, drunken limbs around the parking area, landing punches as best we could, neither of us was getting the better of the other with our fists. I didn't know if I was going to win as I thumped and crashed around, ricocheting off the back of the burger van over and over again, but I wasn't about to give up either.

My opponent must have felt the same way, but he had something I didn't, a Stanley knife. I didn't see him pull it out of his pocket, didn't even see it coming up in his fist until I felt it slashing into my face, cutting the flesh open from my left ear to my neck. It was a few seconds before I felt the pain, by which time the blood had sprayed everywhere as I reeled around, trying to land a return punch, before passing out onto the hard ground.

When I woke up I was in a hospital bed surrounded by nurses and doctors going about their business, giving me blood transfusions and sewing me back up. The blade had cut through some of my facial muscles, which meant that it had half closed my left eye. There was nothing the doctors could do about that, all they did was clean the cut and stitch it up. It was obvious I was going to be left with a big scar, but I'd never been that vain about my appearance so I wasn't too bothered.

The other lad was charged with assault and taken before a jury, but I think the charges were found not to be proven, although the memory is hazy now. I didn't follow the case too closely, not feeling I needed revenge or anything like that. I knew the fight had probably been as much my fault as his, apart from the fact he was carrying a weapon and I wasn't. I just wanted to forget about it and get on with trying to sort out my life.

Many years later things got worse for my left eye when I accidentally put some out-of-date eye drops into it. I'd got some dirt in it from working under the car and I wanted to wash it out. I went to the first-aid kit and found the drops, putting them in without checking the date on the bottle. They must have been lying around for years and had turned to neat acid, burning everything they touched. The pain in my eye socket was instant and the worst I had ever felt, far worse than being slashed. I was rushed to hospital and they pumped gallons of water into the eye, but it was too late and I was left blinded on one side. Thank God it was the already damaged left one and not the remaining good one.

Although many of the things that went wrong in my life were caused by drinking, either by me or by those around me, my habit of going to the pub most evenings also led me to the best thing that ever happened to me. While living in Ashington in 1988 I met Heather in a local bar and that meeting changed my life for ever. The first time I saw her I immediately liked the look of her and wanted to get to know her. I could tell from just chatting in the bar that as well as being attractive she was a decent woman who had led an honest, hard-working life. I dare say I didn't strike her as quite such a good catch and I had to ask her out several times before she agreed to give me a chance. Thank God I persevered and didn't take no for an answer, because the more I got to know her the more wonderful I discovered she was. I got on well with all her friends and family, which felt good since I hardly had anything to do with my own family by then and over the years I hadn't collected any lasting friends of my own.

Somehow I managed to convince her that I wasn't

as bad as my track record might suggest. Our relationship blossomed from there, and we have never looked back. I knew that I had found the love of my life and that if I did anything to mess this one up I would never be given another chance. I had to keep myself out of jail and on the straight and narrow because I couldn't expect someone of Heather's calibre to put up with the sort of lifestyle I had inflicted on Elizabeth and Sandra. I had to finally learn my lesson and take control of my future.

Elizabeth was furious when she discovered I was getting into a new relationship, just as she had been when I started going out with Sandra. Even though our relationship had been over for years by then, she still didn't want any other woman muscling in on what she saw as her territory. She was still living in the Ashington area herself, never having gone back to Scotland after the last time we tried to patch up our marriage, so it was relatively easy for her to interfere in our lives.

Having an angry, jealous ex-wife turning up on her doorstep, or abusing her in the pub, made life hard for Heather and I was really frightened she would decide

I wasn't worth all the trouble. I tried to reason with Elizabeth, then I resorted to shouting at her, but nothing I said had any effect on her behaviour.

In her anger she did everything she could to keep me from seeing the kids, not wanting Heather to have anything to do with them. I guess most mothers feel like that when their ex-husbands start new relationships, hating the idea of the new woman playing happy families with their babies. I wouldn't have minded so much if I had felt that Elizabeth was doing a good job of bringing them up herself, but I had my doubts. For one thing Darren was missing a lot of school, which meant he was falling behind and was having difficulty trying to catch up. I was painfully aware that one of the reasons I had been unable to get a decent job was my lack of education and I hated the idea that the same fate might befall my own children. I knew Heather and I would be much stricter with the kids about things like homework if they lived with us.

Being with Heather changed my whole personality. She was able to calm me down when I was in danger of losing my temper and make me think before I did stupid things. I no longer felt I had to drink to escape being unhappy and I stopped thieving. I was finally starting to turn things around for myself, but there was to be one more hurdle. I found myself in trouble once more, but this time Heather was with me when it happened.

We'd been to visit a friend in prison and the police stopped us for what they said was a routine check at the gates as we came out. We thought we were being picked on but said nothing, staying grimly silent as we allowed them to go through the motions and do whatever they had to do. By the time they had finished and we drove off I was already simmering with repressed anger at being treated like a criminal when I'd done nothing wrong. The feeling only intensified when a mile down the road we were pulled over by another police car. The young policeman from the car was a bit boisterous, I thought, and when he started arguing with Heather I took exception and intervened. There was a scuffle and he got me in a headlock. I felt trapped and memories of the dozens of beatings I'd received at Dale came rushing back, making me panic. I was fighting for breath, desperate to escape from his grip, but the harder I struggled the more tightly he squeezed me and the more I panicked until eventually I sank my teeth into his arm in a last frantic attempt to get loose.

The moment he released me with a shout of pain and I was able to get the air back into my lungs and calm down a little, I realised I'd made a big mistake. Now he really did have a reason to arrest me. I ended up on trial for grievous bodily harm, and was sentenced to seven months for assault. I was furious with myself for making such a bad mistake, and worried that I would lose Heather in the time that I was away. I was terrified that she wouldn't want to have anything to do with someone who was always in so much trouble, and would think that all my promises about staying out of prison were worth nothing. The hurt that I had felt over Sandra's betrayal was still fresh and made me all the more anxious at the thought of what might happen next. If I had lost Heather it would have been the end of the world for me. Just as everything in my life had started to get better I had allowed myself to do something stupid. Maybe if I'd had a clean record up till then the judge would have been more understanding about this one incident, but as it was they just saw an habitual offender back in front of the court yet again.

But Heather was nothing like Sandra. It probably helped that she had actually been there that day and had seen for herself how I had managed to get myself into trouble, and that it had been because I was sticking up for her. I know it would have been very different if I had been caught breaking into premises or stealing a car. But as it was she completely supported me at every stage of the trial and once I was convicted she came to visit me more often than anyone ever had before, turning up at every visiting time and writing me a letter every day. I hardly dared to believe that I had found someone who cared enough to do that for me, and whom I could actually rely on to stick by me and do whatever she promised. By getting myself into trouble I had accidentally put our relationship to the test, and it seemed to be passing with flying colours.

Since serving that sentence I have never had any other trouble with the police, and I hope I never will have again. Heather has brought feelings of peace and order to my life that I had never experienced before.

For the first time I felt that I could have some control over my own destiny, and I grew confident that she would always be there to support me, no matter what. All the urges to draw attention to myself or to lose myself in drink started to fade because she was there to listen to me and comfort me when I felt anxious about things.

Although I was calming down and finally getting some tranquillity in my life, the rest of my family were still battling on in the old way. I was desperately worried about what might happen to Kerry-Anne and Darren and could picture them ending up somewhere like St Margaret's, just as Jocky and I had. More than anything I wanted to save them from having to endure what I had been through at a string of approved schools and borstals. I asked Heather if she would mind having the kids with us full-time, knowing that with her help I might be able to do a decent job of bringing them up. When she said she would be happy to do it I sorted it out with Elizabeth.

Kerry-Anne was about twelve by then and Darren was ten. It would prove to be very hard for Heather to take on the role of their full-time stepmother, harder than I would ever have imagined. She had a daughter of her own, Sarah, who had always been very good and easy to bring up, but my two kids were both resentful and angry by then, and hated any form of discipline or authority. I genuinely wanted to do everything in my power to ensure that they didn't end up leading lives like mine, and I knew that having Heather as a mum was their best chance. If only I'd had someone like her to turn to for love and advice when I was young maybe everything would have been different for me too, but I knew it was a lot to ask of her. I also knew it would affect Sarah's life too, and not necessarily for the better.

Sarah was only just starting her first school when Heather and I got together, and she was soon calling me 'Dad' as if it was the most natural thing in the world. Her own father wasn't on the scene much and I was very happy to take on the responsibility of helping Heather to bring her up, but it made me feel all the sadder that I hadn't been able to play the same sort of role with my own children when they were small. I knew it was asking a lot of both Heather and Sarah to suddenly introduce two troubled young people into our relatively peaceful little family unit. I could still remember how tough it was coming home from St Margaret's and trying to fit in with my brothers and sisters, so I knew it was going to be hard for all of us.

At the time they came to us Darren and Kerry-Anne weren't getting on that well with one another. Sarah and Kerry-Anne, being pretty close in age however, got on well together and Sarah actually got on better with Darren than his own sister did.

Heather and I wanted to do as many things as possible as a family and started to have some great holidays with them at Flamingo Land, a place that Heather had been to before and was keen to introduce me to. To begin with we would take the three kids up for the day, driving up at the crack of dawn, but we never wanted to leave at the end of the day and we used to talk about how nice it would be to be able to stay on the site for a few days and enjoy all the attractions at a more relaxed pace.

So we started saving to bring the kids up for a week at a time. Flamingo Land is a theme park in Yorkshire that started out as a little zoo and then gradually added rides, until now it has some of the biggest and best in the country. It also has acres and acres of caravan parks where holidaymakers can stay. A lot of the caravans are occupied by people who have settled there as well, living the sort of retirement that Heather and I could only dream about at the time.

Before long we were taking the kids there two or three times a year and they always wanted to go back for more. Occasionally we'd try to persuade them to go somewhere new, maybe even to go abroad to get some sun somewhere like Spain or Malta, but they always asked to go back to Flamingo Land, and never wanted to go home once they were there. Heather and I didn't mind because we loved it too, always fantasising about how nice it would be to one day own one of the static caravans and maybe live there all year round. It was only ever a fantasy because we didn't have the money to buy anything, but everyone needs dreams to keep them going.

My other dream was to persuade Heather to marry me. Despite what had happened in my previous marriages, I wanted to be able to believe that we were going to be together for ever, and to do everything I could to make our relationship secure. The day she agreed to be my wife it felt like every prayer I had ever prayed had been answered. I wanted the wedding to be different and romantic, and most of all, unique to us.

Although I'd had my wedding ceremonies in Scotland both times before, I'd never been married in Gretna Green, the village on the west coast of Scotland which is famous historically as a venue for runaway marriages. It was the place where romantic young couples would traditionally go to be married in the blacksmiths' forges without their parents' consent. It all started hundreds of years ago when the laws changed in England, raising the age at which people could marry without consent. The age remained the same in Scotland so kids ran away across the border to tie the knot. At one time boys as young as fourteen and girls as young as twelve would make the trip. Later the law changed in Scotland too and the age limit for marriage rose to sixteen, but parental consent still wasn't needed as it was in England.

Heather and I were hardly two star-crossed kids, but we decided it would be a romantic place to make the relationship official. It was just the two of us at the ceremony, no one else from our past. We were making a new start in life, leaving our pasts behind us but with no idea what difficulties and shocks lay ahead.

Chapter Seventeen

For the first time in my life I was living with someone who liked to keep a nice, clean, orderly home and who looked after everything properly. Being with Heather straightened me out and allowed me to see that I was able to lead a pleasant, normal life just like everyone else. She made me believe that I wasn't inherently bad, as people like Murphy had been telling me all my life, and that I didn't have to feel guilty all the time about things that were now in the past. It was like discovering a new world and I wanted my children to be able to experience the same life, without having to go through the bad stuff I did in order to get there. I wanted them to be able to learn from living with Heather and Sarah and to see what was possible before it was too late and they were trapped in a world of low expectations, low self-esteem and low achievement.

But things are never that simple and people, particularly young people, don't always understand that you have their best interests at heart. Both Kerry-Anne and Darren resented the little bit of discipline that Heather and I insisted on when they came to live with us, and things became increasingly difficult between us, particularly with Darren. I might not have agreed with the violence of the discipline that had been dealt out to me when I was a kid, but I did believe that you had to have rules in any home and they needed to be respected by everyone. Heather agreed, and was doing a great job bringing up Sarah, but applying the same rules to Kerry-Anne and Darren when they were used to doing whatever they pleased wasn't so easy.

We would set curfews that they had to be home by at night and put restrictions on how far away from the house they could go on their own, whereas Elizabeth would pretty much let them do whatever they wanted and go wherever they liked. We would make Darren go to school and then insist that he put in extra hours doing his homework at the end of the school day, hoping he would catch up a bit on all that he'd missed, but every day it was a battle of wills and would end in a shouting match. I could quite understand why Elizabeth, living on her own, had given up the struggle. At least Heather and I could back one another up.

The tensions between us grew worse and worse and once she got to about fifteen, Kerry-Anne announced that she didn't want to live with us any more. She said she wanted to go back to her mother to get away from our rules and to be treated more like an adult. She thought we were being unreasonable with her and went to social services to ask to be moved. In situations like that I suppose the social services have to bow to the wishes of the child unless there is a pressing reason not to, although I never thought they did that for me when I was a boy and needed their help. They agreed to let her go back to Elizabeth. As I watched her return to her old ways I hoped that Kerry-Anne was old enough to look after herself on the street and make sensible decisions, because I felt helpless to do anything more to guide her. There is only so much you can say to a kid before you have to shut up and let them learn their lessons for themselves. I hoped that by having been exposed to a different way of looking at things for a few years she would be able to make better judgements when she needed to, but I knew there was a danger that it wouldn't have been enough. There comes a time with every child, I suppose, when a father has to accept that he can't force them to do anything they don't want to, even if it seems obvious to him that they are making a mistake.

With Kerry-Anne gone, Heather and I did our best to persuade Darren to stay out of trouble. I was still determined to keep him out of the 'bad boys'' schools and away from the paths I had followed for so many years at his age, but by the time he was fourteen or fifteen it was obvious he was falling in with the wrong crowd and I knew I had little chance of influencing him any more. Then someone from security came to our caravan at Flamingo Land during one of our holidays and told us that Darren had been involved in an incident with the slot machines. As a result of that he was banned from the park so we had to cut our holiday short and go home, which was disappointing for all of us and made me both angry with Darren and worried about the path he was following. I didn't seem to be able to make him understand that his behaviour was hurting him as much as anyone else, and I suppose that must have been what everyone had felt when they were trying to find out why I used to do the things I did. I was torn between seeing the dangers lying in wait on the route he was following and knowing that I had been pretty much the same and so could hardly lecture him on his behaviour.

He didn't want to live with us at all after that incident, knowing that his mother would give him greater freedom to do whatever he pleased and wouldn't get on his case every time he got into trouble. It was agreed that he would go back to Elizabeth. He must have been very angry with us because we didn't see him again after that, or even hear from him. He cut us out of his life just as completely as I was always threatening to cut my family out. It was hurtful to think that he felt I had let him down so badly, but I didn't know how to patch things up.

I didn't get to see so much of Kerry-Anne after she left either, but Darren didn't want to have anything to do with us at all. Kerry-Anne would at least come to visit us now and again, giving us no clue as to how she was coping on her own but being perfectly civil while she was with us. We would talk politely for an hour or two, more like acquaintances than family, and I would try not to question her about what was going on in her life, knowing how it annoyed her and how I would worry if I knew too much. Nothing she said to us gave us any idea that she was getting into any sort of trouble, we certainly never saw any signs of drug-taking, but her visits always left me feeling sad that we had become such a small part of her life.

Although I was disappointed that I hadn't been able to help the children escape from their background, it was a relief for Heather and me to finally have time to ourselves. Sarah had also grown up and gone off to live on her own by then and, although she came back to see us regularly, most of the time we were on our own. Ever since the start of our relationship we'd had at least one child with us and had never had a chance to just live as a couple. We now had an opportunity to get to know each other even better and to do some of the things we liked without having to think about what the kids wanted all the time.

We had been on a peaceful break to Flamingo Land on our own when we received a call from friends of Kerry-Anne to say she had died of a heroin overdose in London. The news was so sudden and so unexpected I couldn't take in what they were saying; it was like talking to someone from another planet and I couldn't believe that what I thought I was hearing could be true. We hadn't even known she took drugs and now they were saying she was dead? She'd never said anything to us about going down to London. It was like hearing about some complete stranger. I was so numb with shock that for a while I couldn't even feel the grief. I had prayed so hard for her and Darren to find a different path in life from the rest of our family, wanting them to escape like Jocky had into a better world, where they could amount to something, and now it was too late for Kerry-Anne.

I'd had a bad start but now that I had found Heather I knew it was possible to come through the difficult times and find happiness, but Kerry-Anne would never be able to experience that for herself.

Trying to find out what was going on, we made phone calls to the police in London and I gradually had to accept that the news was true. As the hours passed and I spoke to more and more people, I realised that Kerry-Anne really had gone and that I would never get another chance to try to steer her in a better direction, or even to say goodbye. We had all failed her and I felt terrible.

The police asked us to go to London to identify the body. Heather and I went down to Kentish Town, where Kerry-Anne was laid out at the morgue. For a father or mother to have to see their child dead is one of the hardest things imaginable. It all seemed so wrong and unnatural that she should have gone before me. All I could think was that I wished it was me lying there and not her, and I felt completely powerless to help her or Darren or even myself. Seeing my own child stretched out in a morgue ripped my heart out. It all seemed so stupid and unnecessary, such a waste. All I wanted to do was turn the clock back and try again to explain to her that there was a better way to live your life. I guess every father feels he should be able to protect his children against the dangers of the world, and I'm sure it's always a painful shock for all of us when we discover just how little we can really do for them. And anyway, if I had tried to lecture her about drugs she would probably have turned round and told me I drank too much, and I wouldn't have been able to deny it. But I would have liked a chance to have tried just once more to do the right thing by her.

Once we got to London we started to learn more details of what had happened, piecing the story together and finally getting a more accurate picture of what the last months of Kerry-Anne's short life must have been like. They told us she hadn't been injecting the heroin when she died, she had been 'chasing the dragon'. Apparently that means heating the powder in tinfoil over a cigarette lighter or some other flame, until it turns into a sticky liquid, giving off fumes, which the users inhale. I think it got its name because the liquid wriggles around on the foil like one of those paper dragons the Chinese carry around the streets at festivals and public celebrations. It's a bad name for something so dangerous, making it sound exciting and glamorous rather than sordid and deadly.

Heather and I went back down to the inquest a few weeks later. The coroner said that when they did tests on Kerry-Anne's body they found only minute traces of heroin in her system, but apparently it was a bad batch. She had basically poisoned herself. In the paper a friend of hers was quoted as saying that Kerry-Anne had been trying to cut down on her drug intake. It was a shock to learn so much about my own daughter's life from other people.

I don't know much about drugs, they weren't really available around Kirkcaldy when I was a kid. We had enough troubles with our addictions to drink and cigarettes, we didn't need to go looking for any more. The worst that was available when I was a teenager was a bit of cannabis; there was never any heroin on the streets or anything like that. Drink has caused a lot of problems in my family, soaking up all the money, creating mental and physical health problems, but they are nothing to the problems that drugs can create for families and young kids today.

Once someone gets a taste for a drug like heroin they end up so desperate for money to buy more that they start robbing their own parents and grand-parents, or mugging old ladies in the street. I can't claim I was any sort of angel when I was young, but I was never reduced to doing anything like that. In Ashington now it sometimes seems like all the kids are high on something, even the eight- and nine-year-olds. Over the last two years the drug dealers seem to have taken over the estate where we lived, turning it into a virtual no-go area. There's rubbish all over the place and so many windows are boarded up, hiding God alone knows what secret things that go on inside derelict rooms.

If I had thought that the worst of the ordeal was over and that it was now safe for me to believe I had found out everything and was free to grieve, I was wrong. I kept discovering more about how Kerry-Anne's life had deteriorated after leaving us. Eight or nine months after she died, when I thought I was beginning to get things straight again in my head, I saw a press report claiming that she had been wanted in Newcastle for street robberies, and that was why she had run away to London. Apparently she had fallen in with a boy and the two of them had been robbing folk at knifepoint outside the train station. I guess the police must have known that at the time when we were down in London, but spared me the details. She never got to stand trial, of course, so the case wasn't proven against her, but there was some pretty damning CCTV footage. She and the boy must have needed money to pay for their habit. It seemed that all the efforts Heather and I had made to keep her on the straight and narrow had failed miserably and she had ended up paying the ultimate price by losing her own life. The lad she had been working with eventually went to prison for the crimes they had committed together.

Despite what has happened with Kerry-Anne and Darren, I feel proud to have been a stepfather to Sarah. She has grown up to be a good, settled girl and she and I have always got on well together. Most of the credit for our good relationship must go to Heather, though, she was the one who changed me and made me face my responsibilities as a grown man at last.

Not that I have been a perfect husband or stepfather. Drink was a problem for a long time, sometimes making me aggressive and difficult to live with. Eventually, when I reached the age of fifty, I realised that I had to do something about it if I didn't want to risk driving Heather away like I had driven so many others, and I went on a detox programme. It was a big shock to my body, which I had basically been abusing for nearly forty years, but with Heather's support I managed to give up the drink completely and I haven't touched a drop since. Alcohol has caused so many problems for me and for my family and being without it has transformed everything, allowing me to see the world more clearly and to appreciate everything that I have. Perhaps it was because I was finally finding some peace and happiness that I was able to cope with what happened next and not completely fall to pieces.

Chapter Eighteen

Even though I was living down south in Ashington, I would still take the *Scottish Daily Record* each day. I didn't want to have anything to do with the people from my past or to go back to Scotland, but that didn't mean I wanted to sever all connections. Reading the news from my home country each day was just enough contact for me.

One day my eye was caught by an article that made my heart lurch. As the impact of the words sank in I could feel my chest tightening and I had trouble breathing. Everything was spinning around as I tried to make sense of what was happening.

The Fife police were asking for former residents of

St Margaret's Home who had been there during the sixties and seventies to contact them. The article said the authorities were staging an inquiry regarding the abuse of children in the home during those years.

It was only a short piece but its effect on me was dramatic, like a well-placed hand grenade landing at the base of some giant dam. All the emotions and memories I had been hiding from everyone, including myself, for all those years, suddenly broke free and rushed through the hole left by the explosion, cascading down around me. Unable to cope with the rush of emotion as it swept over me, I started to sob uncontrollably. Hearing the noise Heather came through into the lounge to see if I was all right and was horrified to find me in tears.

'What's happened? What's the matter?' she wanted to know.

But even if I had been able to find the words to explain what I was experiencing, I wouldn't have been able to get them out past the sobbing. I just shook my head, my hands over my face, unable to say even a word as my entire past flashed before me in every gruesome detail.

'Whatever is the matter?' Heather asked again, her face filled with concern as I continued to sob.

She sat beside me and put her arm around my shoulders, holding me tight, obviously shocked and frightened at not knowing what could have happened to reduce me to such a state in a matter of minutes, assuming that I had received some terrible news and anxious to know what it could be. Seeing the paper open in front of me she picked it up and read the article while she waited for me to gather myself together. I kept on sobbing as her eyes scanned the print. She gave a sharp intake of breath and her hand covered her mouth as she realised that this was the home I had been in, that these events must have had something to do with me.

The inside of my head was filled with dozens of different pictures, all jostling for space as the memories of those terrible ordeals in Murphy's bed came back to me. I relived being lifted from my own bed and carried down those dark corridors and then the long, humiliating, painful hours that I had had to spend with him, forced to let him do whatever he wanted, crying out and nobody hearing. It was like watching film clips from someone else's life as I saw what he, a grown man like I was now, was doing to little Tommy. Part of me wanted to stop the images immediately, to go back to the state of forgetfulness that I had been existing in for so long, but it was too late. Now that the floodgates were open there was nothing I could do to stem the torrent of horror. I knew it was me I was watching, but it had been so long since my brain had allowed me to see the pictures that they seemed to show another person from another time, like a ghost from my past.

My overwhelming emotion as I watched those pictures was guilt. I felt that everything that had happened to me at St Margaret's had been my fault, just as everything that had happened in my life after that had been down to me and the bad choices I had made at almost every turn. I had allowed Murphy to do those things to me, so I was guilty. I had been a bad boy and I had deserved all the punishments and all the pain that I had received at Dale. I had deliberately gone out and committed crimes and I had deserved every prison sentence I had ever received. I had been a terrible husband and father and now Kerry-Anne was dead and my son no longer wanted anything to do with me, and that felt like it was all my fault too.

Seeing that article in the paper made me feel that the police were now coming after me. They had discovered what a naughty boy I was all those years ago and were trying to hunt me down in order to punish me. Part of me knew that was an irrational fear, but knowing that didn't make the feeling any less real or frightening.

The next emotion that swept over me was relief at seeing the words written in black and white, knowing that it meant someone else might actually be going to believe me if I told them what had happened to me all those years ago, when I was so young and vulnerable. I also felt like I might finally begin to understand why I was the way I was, and would learn more about the parts of my childhood that I had allowed to slip away into oblivion. My tears were also tears of sadness for what had happened to little Tommy as the memories flooded back into my mind, images I hadn't conjured up for decades. For the first time in years I was seeing Murphy again for what he truly was and I knew that this investigation must be about him.

Heather was still by my side, growing more and more desperate for me to talk to her, to tell her what was wrong, what it was about the news story that had upset me so deeply, but I still couldn't find the words I needed, just wanting her to hold me tight until I had cried myself dry.

Then I felt a familiar fear returning, warning me that if I did step forward and talk about what had happened to me during that time I would still not be believed. Murphy's taunts came echoing back down the years to me.

'You've been a liar since the day you were born! No one will believe you.'

I remembered how I had written to him from prison, trusting him to tell me about myself and my life, forgetting that he was the cause of everything that had gone wrong, almost delivering myself up into his hands again.

Everything I had done with my life since then suggested that his predictions had been right. I'd been such a bad boy through the years; first the approved school, then the borstal and the prison sentences, the thieving and broken marriages, the alienation from my family, even the death of Kerry-Anne. All these things seemed to show just what a wicked person I was. I'd been in virtually every type of institution and hardly ever held down a decent job for more than a few weeks. Why would the police and the authorities take any notice of me now when I had such a terrible track record? Why would they take the word of someone like me against that of someone like Murphy or the many social workers and psychologists whom I had come up against over the years?

After what seemed like an age I was able to get control of the sobbing and my chest stopped heaving, leaving me feeling drained and exhausted, my heart thumping in my ears. Heather was still there with her arm around me, waiting patiently for me to be in a fit state to be able to talk to her, to explain what was happening. The pictures in my head were settling down into patterns, no longer flashing up at random but starting to take on a form and shape: I was gradually remembering more and more of the connecting pieces of the jigsaw that held them together and which told the whole sad tale of little Tommy Wilson's early years.

Very, very slowly and haltingly I told Heather the story of the first decade of my life, having to take deep breaths after every few words just to be able to keep going. For the first time ever I was revealing to someone else the secrets that I had been keeping even from myself for forty years. Even though I could see from the newspaper article that there was now a good chance the police would listen to me and believe me, I still didn't want to phone them. I was frightened that I would pour my heart out to them only to have them turn round and tell me they didn't believe me. What if they asked me to prove that Murphy had done those things to me? How would I ever be able to do that after so long? The thought that I might open up my heart and then be told I was a liar was terrifying. To speak about such things was going to be humiliating enough, without then having doubt cast on whether I was telling the truth.

My relationship with the police had always been one of them arresting or questioning me and me being in the wrong. They had always been the authority figures in my life, almost as much as Murphy had been when I was a child. The thought of going to them made me feel like a child again, as if I was telling tales to one adult about another. Murphy was an ex-policeman himself, so didn't that mean they were bound to take his side?

It just didn't feel right to be considering actually delivering myself into the hands of any authorities, least of all the police. Thanks to Heather's good influence I had been doing so well at staying out of their way over the previous few years, and the thought of having anything to do with them again made me feel sick.

Heather had a different view. Always having been a law-abiding citizen she wasn't afraid of the police, seeing them as being on her side in most situations, rather than as agents of some invisible enemy. It seemed obvious to her, as she listened with increasing horror to my tales from the past, that I should respond to the article and ring them immediately in order to tell them everything I knew about Murphy. Having heard what he had done she seemed to want to see him brought to justice even more than I or the police did. When I actually put into words some of the things that he had done to me it sounded even more shocking and evil than when I saw it as flashbacks in my head. I could see that she was deeply shaken and angry at the thought of someone in his position abusing his power so cruelly.

Heather held me and comforted me. It must have been frightening for her to see me crumbling in front of her eyes like a frightened little boy. She tried to persuade me to make the call, but I was in too much of a state to be reasoned with at that moment, an emotional wreck from the shock of having so much of my past suddenly dug up and paraded across my memory. She could see that by badgering me to make the call she was likely to make me even more stubborn and so she fell silent, just offering me comfort and a listening ear, wisely biding her time.

But she wasn't going to give up that easily. The next morning, once I had calmed down after a long, sleepless night, and had had some time to reflect on everything, she went back to encouraging me to make the call. I still didn't want to, but she was persistent and in my heart I knew she was right. To remain silent now that I knew someone was asking questions would have been cowardly. I realised that Murphy must have been abusing other boys as well as me, otherwise the story would never have got out to the police, and I would be betraying the others as well as letting down my childhood self if I didn't step forward and tell them what I knew. But knowing I should do it, and actually finding the courage to pick up the phone, were two very different things. I told Heather to stop nagging me and fell into a deep, thoughtful silence as I tried to sort everything out in my head.

Of course Heather didn't stop nagging for long, because she was certain it was the right thing to do, but it wasn't until two days after I had first read the article that she finally managed to convince me to phone the number the police had given out in the paper. All through those two days I was continually finding myself overwhelmed with emotion and unable to hold back the tears as more memories of little Tommy and Murphy came back to me. The thought of possibly having to confront Murphy face to face made me physically shake, like I was that small, helpless boy again, bracing myself to take a beating. I was sure he would deny every accusation I made and I would be branded a liar by everyone, like he had always predicted. He would be mocking me, just as he always had, for daring to even think that I could challenge him. I wasn't sure either how I would cope with the whole world knowing the humiliating facts about what he had done to me. Did I really want my family and friends to know that I had been used like that?

Eventually I accepted that Heather was right and that I had no option but to try to make Murphy pay for what he had done; I had to make the call or my mind would never be at peace and I would always be feeling I had failed the other boys. Although the anger at what Murphy had done to me was building up inside me I still didn't want to talk about what had happened to me in front of Heather or Sarah, even though Heather now knew most of the truth. I wasn't even sure I was going to be able to find the words I needed to describe the experiences I'd had as a child when I finally had to spit them out, so I went upstairs to make the call, closing the bedroom door behind me, wanting to be alone and private when at last I lifted the lid on my past and allowed it to escape into the outside world.

I took several deep breaths, my heart thumping in my throat, then picked up the phone and dialled.

Chapter Nineteen

The policeman at the other end of the phone line was businesslike but friendly, asking two or three simple questions just to make sure he was talking to someone who genuinely had been at St Margaret's during the period they were interested in. They must have had a list of our names and once he was sure that I was the Tommy Wilson on that list he became even friendlier.

'We would like to interview you as soon as possible, sir,' he said, politely.

I felt encouraged by his tone and two days later I travelled up to Glenrothes police station. If I had been frightened of making the phone call, I was even more terrified of the thought of talking to someone face to face, and appalled that the world was now going to learn all the details of what had happened to little Tommy Wilson. But I wanted them to realise that Tommy hadn't chosen his way of life, and that the scars I was still carrying inside me had been caused by Murphy. At least on the phone they couldn't see me; now I was going to have to look them in the eye as I spilled out my terrible secrets.

Heather kindly agreed to come with me, just as she had when I was up for trial for assaulting the policeman. I think she could see how nervous I was and how much I needed her support. I had never had anyone in my life who had been willing to put themselves out for me in the way Heather did. Mum and Dad hardly ever bothered to visit me when I was locked up anywhere, and both Elizabeth and Sandra had eventually lost interest in me when the going got too tough, but Heather didn't seem to question for a second that her place was by my side and always would be. Murphy had told me so often how no one loved me but him that it was consoling to know that Heather was there for me and that she believed me completely. If someone as good as Heather could love me, I reasoned, I couldn't be as bad as everyone else seemed to think.

Even though the policeman had been so understanding on the phone, and even though I now knew I wasn't the only one to have suffered at Murphy's hands, the idea of having to put into words the memories that I had obviously forced myself to forget for so long, and have them recorded and written down, was terrifying. I knew that once I had taken this step I would be committed to carrying on down a path that was likely to lead to me having to see Murphy again.

It still seemed impossible to me that I could ever say anything against Murphy to anyone without some sort of retribution. He was 'Uncle Dave', wasn't he? The man everyone treated like God at St Margaret's; the man who could do whatever he wanted to whoever he wanted, whenever he wanted. It was still a struggle to imagine being able to find the courage to stand up to such an authority figure, even though I was an adult and he must be a frail, elderly man by now. So many thoughts were going through my head, confusing and frightening me, making me wish I had never started out on the journey, that I had just ignored the newspaper and locked my memories back up in the box where they had been living for so long, so that they would leave me alone. But maybe by letting them out I would reach some sort of peace that I had never been able to find before.

Maybe this would be like a kind of exorcism, driving the bad spirits and the bad memories out once and for all into the light. If I could help to bring Murphy to justice and have him imprisoned for his crimes then he would no longer be the great authority figure in my life, he would no longer be able to strike fear into my heart every time I thought about him or imagined him telling me off.

Heather stayed with me right through the interview at the police station. I didn't want her to leave. I'd been told I would be interviewed by an inspector, but when we got there we discovered it would actually be a CID detective and a policewoman.

I felt a twinge of panic when I saw that there was going to be another woman in the room. It was too late to turn round and go home, and I didn't have the courage to speak up and ask if I could talk to male officers only because I didn't like the idea of talking about such intimate things in front of any woman other than Heather. It seemed like I was being stupid but I couldn't help the way I felt. I was pretty sure I could force myself to talk about most of what had happened, but I was afraid I just wouldn't be able to bring myself to admit that I had ever been penetrated by Murphy if there was another woman listening and watching me.

The room was pretty bare, with just a long table and six chairs to furnish it. As the four-hour interview progressed they asked me about every detail of my life, wanting me to explain as accurately as possible how Murphy came and took me from my bed, to describe the terrible things he did to me in his room. I felt horribly uncomfortable, and was unable to stop the tears. I could almost physically see the vital question coming towards me, making my mouth go dry and my brain freeze. When it was finally spoken out loud I could feel all their eyes on me, patiently waiting in the silence for me to reply. I knew they wanted me to tell the truth and I knew they wanted to be able to convict

Murphy for as many of his crimes as possible, but at that final moment, when the question was spoken out loud – 'Did Murphy penetrate you?' – I denied it. I just couldn't face the thought that they would know he had done that to me.

I wasn't trying to protect Murphy at all; that was the last thing I wanted to do. I was lying to protect myself from the final embarrassment and humiliation, the final admission that as a child I had been no more than an object to be raped and pushed aside. I did drop hints as I told my story, talking to them about having a sore bottom in the classroom at school the following day, but when confronted with a blunt question I denied that any penetration had taken place. My brain wanted to say 'Yes', but my mouth wouldn't allow me to speak the word. Considering how much of the abuse I was willing to talk about, it was a ridiculous thing to be unable to admit, but somehow it would have felt like denying my own manhood.

I was horrified by my failure to speak honestly because it meant that even after all those years Murphy still had the power to make me betray myself, to make me feel like I had been in the wrong. I was still allowing myself to feel ashamed of my childhood, and of how I became a habitual petty criminal later in my life. And behind all that lay the terrible truth that I was still ashamed that I had allowed him to do those things to me. Even as I was denying it I felt sick at the thought that I might be letting Murphy get away with something; that I might be letting down both myself and all the other boys who had suffered at his hands.

As soon as the denial was out of my mouth I wanted to shout out a correction, but it was too late. To change my story once it had been told would have suggested I wasn't telling the whole truth; that I was, as Murphy had always said, a liar. I had trapped myself.

The police told us that the investigation had got under way because someone else had reported Murphy for abusing them. They admitted it wasn't the first time he had been reported to the police, but it was the first time they had got as far as talking to other potential witnesses and the first time they had set out to prosecute him. In 1970 some boys who had been at St Margaret's after me had found the courage to report Murphy to their social workers for whatever he was doing to them. The allegations were passed by those social workers to the police, but there was no record of the boys being interviewed. Without a formal complaint, the police told us, nothing could be done to prevent Murphy from continuing to work with children.

In the seventies many people were still in denial about the scale of abuse going on in children's homes. The possibility that such things were happening seemed so shocking and abhorrent that no one wanted to think about it; everyone wanted to brush the subject quickly out of sight under the carpet. That was how people like Murphy were able to get away with such things all their lives. It was one of those secrets that no one liked to talk about, or even admit existed. As long as child abuse remained a forbidden subject, too disgusting to even be mentioned in polite society, it was impossible to expose what was going on.

The authorities must have believed there was at least a possibility that those boys in 1970 were telling the truth because they did temporarily move Murphy away from temptation, putting him to work in an old people's home instead. When the case never came to court, however, he must have managed to persuade them that that meant he was innocent, that the accusations were false, because it wasn't long before he had managed to wangle his way back into another children's home and had started abusing boys there in just the same way.

This time, however, it seemed the police and the local authorities were taking the accusations more seriously and wanted to ensure they got him convicted. It felt like a huge weight had been lifted off me as I talked to them about Murphy as the bad guy after so many years. For the first time ever I felt that I was on the good side in a fight and I wanted to do all I could to help the police convict Murphy, which made me feel all the worse for lying about the penetration.

Since starting the new investigation the police told us they had interviewed three hundred and twenty-five witnesses and received forty-four complaints against Murphy as a result. By the time I came into their investigation they had been hearing the stories of other children who had been in the home for a couple of years, gradually piecing all the different descriptions together, seeing the patterns of his behaviour emerging and following up leads. It seemed strange to think that all that had been going on while I had known nothing about it. Some of the other witnesses were names that I remembered from when I was at St Margaret's, including one who was a couple of years older than me but had been very small as a boy, seeming younger than his age. He had also been one of the boys who tried to lodge a complaint in 1970 as well, which would have been about the time when he was leaving St Margaret's.

He later told me that he had moved away to Liverpool and had eventually done well for himself, even becoming a lay magistrate. Determined not to let Murphy get away with his crimes just because so many of them were now a long way in the past, he had gone back to report what had happened to Fife Council, who had suggested he go to his local police station. Times had changed since 1970 and everyone was more willing to listen to people with stories of being abused and to believe them. The police in Liverpool did just that. They had then contacted the

Scottish police, who had set an inquiry into Murphy's activities in motion, getting statements from as many former residents as possible.

In his statement, this one particular boy talked about Murphy tying him to the bed and spitting on him, which I don't remember him doing to me, so I guess there must have been a lot of other things which took place in that bedroom as well as the tortures I had to endure. His relationship with each of us must have been different and his fantasies about us very varied. When I think how many frightened little boys must have suffered the same fate as me after I left, it makes my blood run cold and the tears come back to my eyes even now.

Despite the fact that he had ended up being so successful in life, in his statement the other ex-St Margaret's boy said that he had been deeply damaged by the abuse he received from Murphy. In his confusion he had spent a few years working as a rent boy in London before managing to get his life straight and on track. He said he had never suffered psychiatric problems in the long term, or turned to drink or drugs, but like me he had suffered periods of depression.

Another man, whom I don't remember as a boy, had also filed a complaint against Murphy and claimed he had been abused at two other Fife homes, Greenbanks and Ovenstone, both of which I had spent time in as a small child. This made me wonder if things had happened to me when I was too tiny even to be able to understand what was going on or to remember anything.

I don't know if the police would have been able to track me all the way down to Ashington if I hadn't spotted that article in the paper, but they told me they had got as far as knocking on Jocky's door in Kirkcaldy and interviewing him. The police said that he told them he had never had any trouble from Murphy or any other member of staff at St Margaret's.

It was two years from the start of their investigation before the police felt they had gathered together enough evidence from us all to finally charge Murphy. They wanted to be entirely sure that their case would stand up before they brought it, knowing that if he escaped this time they might never have another chance to bring him to justice. In some ways I'm glad that I didn't know anything about it until right at the end because living with the returned memories for two years, knowing that Murphy was still free and might be able to get away with his crimes, would have been hard. As it was, he appeared at court quite soon after I had given my statement to the police.

The tables had turned dramatically and the man who had been treated like a sort of god for so much of his life was now accused of being more like the devil himself. My great fear now was that he would be so confident and plausible in court, just as he had always been when he was ruling St Margaret's, that the judge would be as fooled by him as every other adult had been throughout his life. I wanted to do everything I could to help in the fight to bring him to justice, but at the back of my mind lurked the uncomfortable knowledge that I hadn't told the whole truth, and in my lie I might have left him a loophole that he would be able to escape through at the last moment.

Chapter Twenty

It was forty years since I had last seen Murphy, since I had been banished from St Margaret's to the brutality of Dale for the crimes of catching a bus home and stealing half a crown. In my mind I pictured he was going to look the same as he had done on the day I last saw him as I was sent to Dale; I couldn't imagine how the passing years might have changed him, as they had certainly changed me. Nor could I imagine how I would feel when he was actually standing in front of me.

For three decades my life had gone virtually nowhere, just a steady slide downhill from one disaster to another, until I finally met Heather and my luck had started to turn. The years had treated Murphy very differently. Not only did he have the respect of virtually everyone who knew about him but did not know the secrets of his night-time activities, he had also ended up as quite a wealthy man, owning several properties.

I suppose never having married or had children of his own, and always working, he had managed to save all his earnings and invest them in property. Nor did he drink or indulge in any of the other bad habits that drain the money out of the pockets of men like me.

He still lived in one of his houses in St Monans, a little fishing village further along the Fife coast. I think he had even owned the same house when I was at St Margaret's, so he had probably been able to buy it very cheap, at a time before anyone had ever heard of a property boom in Scotland.

The local people in St Monans, knowing nothing about his secret life, thought so highly of him they were actually in the process of erecting a statue of him in honour of all the work he had done with children over the years, both at St Margaret's and at the home where he was given another job after being allowed back from working in the old people's home.

Like so many before, these people were blind to the true nature of Murphy. He had used his position of power to conceal the cruel, sadistic and disturbed streak in his character. He played up his saintly role and everyone fell for it. It made me wonder what secrets and lies lay behind all the other statues you see dotted around cities and towns: the generals who won great battles, the politicians who created new laws, the saints who founded orphanages and saved souls, did they all have as many things to hide as Murphy?

When the accusations of child abuse first started to emerge about him, everyone who knew Murphy found it impossible to believe that a man who had been a policeman, worked with the social services and looked after so many troubled young people for so long could be the same man who was being described as a predatory monster by the boys he was supposed to be looking after. He was a convincing con man, able to make people believe whatever he wanted them to believe about him. But as the accusations mounted up even his most loyal supporters had to accept that there was something wrong, something that needed to be investigated, if only to clear his name. He was even being accused of abusing children outside the homes where he worked, whom he had managed to lure into his house in St Monans, bringing the scandal and controversy right into the heart of their community. They might have been able to turn a blind eye to accusations of misbehaviour from the past in some children's home they knew nothing about, but to have it happening in a house in their own village shocked them into taking more notice of the allegations.

Perhaps if he had been a weak man it might have been possible to find some pity for him and some understanding for his inability to be able to resist temptation when it was left in his way. But he was anything but weak. It is my belief that right from the start of his career Murphy had deliberately worked his way into a position where he would have almost unlimited access to vulnerable young boys, a position that would give him the power to act as he pleased and live out the evil fantasies he had always harboured. With Murphy, everything was calculated and dangerously considered.

I didn't get to see him until we were actually in the same courtroom. It was hard to imagine that the sad, frail old man who shuffled out into the court below us was the same person as the vigorous young man who had ruled our lives so totally for so many years. If I had passed him in the street I would never have given a second glance to the bald old man with tufts of grey hair sticking out at each side of his head, thick glasses and a walking stick. It was terrible to think that even in his old age he had continued to abuse young boys, which must have been even more alien and repellent for the victims than how it was for us, when he was a young and fit man.

There were several of us St Margaret's boys in the courtroom, craning our necks to see. As Murphy entered he very deliberately looked up at all of us sitting in the back gallery, giving us a friendly wave before settling down. When he was asked later by the policeman who was escorting him why he had done that, he said he wanted to see how 'his boys' had grown up. When the policeman told me that I felt sick and couldn't stop myself from crying. In Murphy's mind it seemed we still were 'his boys', almost like he owned us. How did he live with his conscience, knowing what he had done to us and how his actions had blighted our lives?

To many people, myself included, just two years before that simple statement would have sounded so innocent, even admirable, coming from a man who truly cared about the lads put in his charge. But in these changed circumstances it now seemed evil and calculated, like we were still his possessions even after all these years, still somehow within his sphere of influence, objects for him to do with as he pleased. I remembered the letters he had written me when I was in prison, the way in which he had continued to show what could have been seen as a paternal concern for me, even though I was by then a young man. I felt so many conflicting emotions at the same time all I wanted to do was cry.

When the case got under way I had to go to court twice to give evidence, once in Perth High Court and once in Glasgow. Murphy never showed any remorse or respect towards any of his former victims. As the charges were being read out he sat in the box, shaking his head back and forth as if denying everything. He must have known by the time they came to court that the police had a watertight case against him, because at the last minute he decided to strike a deal rather than trying to protest that he was innocent of all charges. He agreed to plead guilty to thirty-eight of the charges against him, around half of the total.

One of the charges he pleaded guilty to was 'on various occasions between 15 May 1960 and 31 December 1966 you did use lewd indecent and libidinous practices or behaviour towards Thomas Stewart Wilson . . . then a child in your care and protection, and put your private member between his thighs and rubbed yourself against him to the emission of semen.'

How odd and clinical it sounded when phrased like that, conveying none of the fear, confusion and disgust I had felt at the time that it happened in that darkened room.

He also pleaded guilty to charges of buggery against three other boys, so the question of whether or not he had penetrated me became irrelevant to the police case as they had enough to convict him, and I was spared from having to answer questions about it in court. Murphy had denied penetrating me, although he had admitted abusing me. There seemed no rhyme or reason as to which of the charges he decided to admit to and which he decided to deny. There were some boys who turned up to be witnesses and he denied touching them at all. I have no doubt that he did whatever it was they were accusing him of, because I know how much he lied about what he did to me. It is so traumatic to come forward and give evidence on a subject like that that I can't imagine any of his alleged victims were making their accusations up. No one would want to put themselves through such an ordeal voluntarily.

The way in which he picked and chose which charges to plead guilty to made it seem as if it was just a game to him, a sport like all the others that he used to revel in as a young man. It seemed very wrong that he was allowed to get away with it, but I suppose if they had challenged him on each charge the case would have gone on for years and he might have died before they were able to convict him of anything. But it still made me angry. As I watched him looking up at us I was sure that he remembered exactly what he had done to me, so why should he get away with denying it? But still I couldn't find the voice to tell the truth and denounce him that one final time.

At the end of the trial he was found guilty of so many charges that the outcome was not really affected by his denial of some of them, but it meant that the fact that he had penetrated me was still my own guilty secret.

I was disappointed that he had been allowed to get away with lying about so many things, and said so to the social worker who had been assigned to help me.

'But in the end, Tom,' she said, 'he will be judged.'

I suppose she was talking about the final judgement when he reached the gates of heaven, which is fair enough if you have faith that that will happen. There have been periods of my life when I would have been able to believe that there was a God watching over me, but gradually my faith had been eroded with every new thing that went wrong. I finally stopped believing in God about ten years ago; since then I have been out of trouble and out of prison, which makes you wonder whether there might be any connection.

In February 2001 Murphy was sentenced to fifteen years and just from looking at how frail he was I could see it was unlikely he would live long enough to ever be free again. I knew from experience how hard prison life could be for a young, fit man, let alone one whose health was already fading and who would be labelled as a paedophile. He was wearing a charcoal grey suit and stumbled in the dock as Lord Hardie, the judge, read out the sentence. He looked shocked, as if he had still imagined he might get away with it, as if he had believed they wouldn't dare to lock him up after all he had done for the community over the years. He had been invincible for so long he obviously found it hard to believe that he might actually be going to have to serve his penance.

'Your victims were just children,' Lord Hardie told him, 'who required help, but instead you abused your position of trust to inflict damage on them over a period between 1960 and 1986. The damage you have done to these people and their pain and suffering cannot be overstated.'

There were a lot of us up in the gallery and we

cheered as the sentence was pronounced, and one or two of the others actually clapped their hands, and shouted abuse at him as he was led away. I stayed silent, still finding it hard to verbally express any emotion as tears ran down my cheeks in a mixture of relief, joy and sadness. I was happy that he had been sentenced, although fifteen years seemed lenient compared to the lifetimes of misery that he had inflicted on so many of us. He would almost certainly never taste freedom again, which could only be good news, but I thought it unfair that he might die before even half his sentence had been served. I had moved on a long way since the day that I first read the article in the *Daily Record* and began to piece together my forgotten past, but I still felt that I had somehow been cheated of a just retribution.

The day of the sentence in the Glasgow High Court we had all been taken there in a bus laid on by social services. I got into conversation with one of the social workers on the way.

'Do you realise,' he said, 'you could go to the courts yourself and get compensation for what Murphy did to you?'

It had never occurred to me that I could do such a thing. It had only been a few months since I had even been able to talk to anyone about what had happened; this would be another giant step forward for me, shouting out the truth for the whole world to hear. He explained that if I wanted to pursue that line I needed to find myself a suitable lawyer.

A week after returning to Ashington, having seen Murphy brought down, I decided that I wanted to go through with it and I went to see a local solicitor. He said he thought I had a good case for compensation. For eight months he corresponded with the Scottish courts, before eventually telling me he couldn't take the case himself because it had to be held in the Court of Sessions in Edinburgh and an English lawyer would not be allowed to go into a Scottish court to defend me.

Annoyed that he had wasted so much time before telling me this vital fact, I went back to the Scottish solicitor, Richard McFarlane, from the firm of Rollo Davidson McFarlane in Crossgates, Cupar, who had defended me for around ninety per cent of the cases that I had been involved in throughout my life. He is now a Sheriff in one of the courts and has done well for himself. He had always been very sympathetic to me, even when I kept reoffending without being able to give him any explanation as to why I was doing it. Now, at last, I was able to tell him something about myself which explained so much about why I had been the way I was as a young man.

I have thought a lot about how my brain managed to suppress the memories of those nights with Murphy for so long, and I have talked to psychologists and psychiatrists since I became aware of this. They tell me it is quite a common occurrence. It seems that sufferers from child abuse react in a similar way to soldiers who have been through traumatic experiences in war. It's all part of what they call the post-traumatic stress syndrome. When the brain is unable to cope with the enormity of what its owner has experienced, it simply ignores it.

There used to be veterans of the trenches in the First World War who would never talk about what they had seen and suffered. It was like they had wiped the pictures from their brains and they didn't want to run the risk of bringing them back. Children who have been badly abused can sometimes be affected in the same way, but the result is different because of the secrecy that surrounds every individual case. Everyone knew that the First World War had taken place, and could imagine how each person in it might have suffered. But if an abused child is persuaded to remain silent about his or her experiences no one other than the abuser will ever know about them, until a particular trigger sets the memories off, or until the victim's mind feels able to cope with the pain of remembering and of bringing back those pictures. To this day I have still not discussed anything to do with Murphy or St Margaret's with anyone in my own family, although I have talked to some of Heather's friends and family.

I have no way of knowing if Murphy understood this and believed it would protect him, or if he thought that his victims would simply be too afraid to speak out about what we remembered, or whether he was just hoping that if we did speak out we wouldn't be believed. But all the time that we remained silent and forgetful he was able to continue taking vulnerable small boys to his bed and doing whatever he wanted to them.

'I truly believe, Tom,' Richard said when I'd finished telling my story, 'that that was where it all went wrong for you.'

Chapter Twenty-One

Murphy was found dead in his cell in Peterhead Prison in June 2003, after serving just two years of his fifteen-year sentence. The coroner reported that he had died of natural causes. The fact that he only spent such a small part of his life behind bars leaves me feeling cheated, but I'm glad that he died in Peterhead, which had been turned into a sex offenders' prison by then, because that was the prison where I served my longest sentence, and where I had written to Murphy as an adult. It seemed like a sort of poetic justice that he should die alone in one of the cells where I had been so wretched myself.

Maybe if he hadn't treated me so callously in

those early years of my life I would have turned out to be a different person. Maybe I would have been an honest, hard-working citizen, like I always wanted to be. Maybe I would even have made a success of my life, like Jocky did. Maybe everything that went wrong wasn't all my fault after all. That is a momentous thought when you have spent nearly half a century believing that you are a bad person.

The fact that Murphy had been convicted and gone to jail, however, did not mean that my ordeal was over. Now that the memories had escaped and were swirling wildly around in my head day and night, there was no chance of getting them back into their box. While the investigation and the trial had been under way I had had something to think about, somewhere to channel my anger, but once it was all over I was still left with the mental pictures and psychological scars. I knew that I was going to need professional help if I wasn't to succumb to new levels of depression and self-loathing, and risk driving Heather away with my moods. The elation at seeing Murphy put away was soon replaced by a terrible emptiness when I looked back across the wreckage of my life to my ruined childhood.

In my struggle to avoid descending into the black pit of despair I tried ringing one of the well-known helplines for child abuse, wanting someone to pour it all out to, someone to talk me out of committing suicide. A man's voice answered and encouraged me to start talking. Once I started there was no stopping me and the memories and thoughts just kept flooding out of my mouth. I was on the phone for an hour and twenty minutes in the end, just talking, with him listening and giving me the odd grunt of encouragement.

Then suddenly it all seemed stupid to me, he was just letting me ramble on and saying nothing. I could hear my own voice going on and on and it was like I was talking to myself. I hung up and never phoned a helpline again.

After Murphy had been found guilty several people came forward and apologised to us all on behalf of the council and the community for everything that we had been through. It felt good to finally have it recognised that maybe not everything that went wrong in my life was my fault. It was also good to hear them admitting that the adults of the time had a responsibility to ensure that children like me were cared for with kindness and consideration, and that they had failed in that responsibility. But in the end they were only words. These were different people to the ones who were making those decisions at the time I was a child. I also felt they could still have been doing more to help the others who have not yet had their stories listened to, but at least it is a start and an acceptance that people like me aren't making these things up as some sort of excuse for later failures. I didn't have to feel guilty or ashamed any more, because it wasn't all my fault. Part of the blame had to lie with Murphy and the council who put little Tommy Wilson into the care of such a man.

Although Murphy had been publicly exposed and denounced, that wasn't going to help me in any material way. It wasn't going to recompense me for all the years of unhappiness and all the depression and all the long nights I spent in solitary confinement in prison, wasting my life away. Fife Council was offering several thousand pounds to each of his victims, if we signed agreements not to talk about what had happened to us when we were in their care. I didn't think that a few thousand pounds was nearly enough and I certainly didn't intend to sign any gagging order. It was my life and I wanted to be able to talk about it to whoever was willing to listen and in whatever manner I wanted.

For over forty years I had been keeping the secret, even from myself, allowing the truth to fester away in some hidden recess of my brain, doing untold damage. Now that I had uncovered it and exposed it to the light I was certainly not willing to pack it away out of sight again, just to save the blushes of a few council officials. People like Murphy thrive in a culture of secrecy, where victims are persuaded not to talk about their experiences. This should never be allowed to continue.

I don't think at that stage it had occurred to me that I would ever write this book about my experiences, but I still wanted to defend my rights to talk about my childhood should I wish to. After all the years of saying nothing and of being told that if I did speak I wouldn't be believed, I didn't think that it was fair for me to be silenced now.

I knew that Fife Council had the power to make more generous amends for the damage they had caused me as long as I didn't sign anything, so I refused their offer and Richard, my lawyer, went ahead with bringing my case to court in order to try to get the sort of settlement that might help Heather and me to have at least a little peace of mind together in our later years.

I travelled back to Kirkcaldy and went to the council's records office in search of all my files; partly because I wanted to have every possible scrap of ammunition at my fingertips by the time the case opened, and partly because I wanted to satisfy my own curiosity about the bits of my childhood that I couldn't remember. I wanted to find out everything possible about what had happened to little Tommy during those dark years, to reclaim my own child-hood so that I could start to put it all into some sort of healthier perspective.

I half expected to get to the records office and be told that all my papers had been lost or destroyed. I had heard so many stories from other people about how their files mysteriously went missing at the moment they went to look for them. If that had happened I don't know if I would have believed those responsible, or whether I would have suspected them of trying to cover their tracks. But the files were all still there, yellowing and dusty, the paper stiffened with age. I carried them to a desk like they were gold dust, and felt almost breathless as I sat down to study them, steeling myself for feelings and emotions I hadn't experienced for nearly half a century.

Reading through them was like watching a film about someone else, a small boy who grew up in the 1950s and 60s, a very different world to today's. I was stepping through a door into another world, one that immediately became familiar as the notes jogged new memories that had been buried deep in my subconscious.

When I dug further I found reports about how the police had been trying to put together a case of child abuse against Gibson, the man who had run the home before Murphy, and I read how he had died before they were able to take him to court and make him answer the charges. I could dimly remember Gibson bathing me when I was about four years old, and carefully washing my private parts with his soapy fingers, but I couldn't remember anything else happening. It had always seemed like a fairly normal thing to do if you are washing a small child, but I suppose such routines could easily have led on to other things with the older children. A mother would certainly wash her baby like that, and maybe some fathers would too. But at what stage would they stop and begin to teach the child to do it themselves? And is it ever right for a man who is not the child's father to do it? There were so many grey areas and question marks and doubts.

I was able to trace ninety per cent of my life in those musty files, and seeing my progress recorded through the eyes of others opened my own eyes. Many of the things that had puzzled me in the past started falling into place and I began to understand why I was the way I was. I could understand why, if people had been interfering with me from before I could remember, I might have started to retreat into a daydreaming state as a little boy on the beach. It's something that I still find myself doing today, becoming lost in my own thoughts, drifting away from the complicated, threatening world around me to a safer place where I am on my own and no one can get to me or hurt me or let me down.

I didn't have as much luck in tracing my medical history. None of the GPs I had visited in the first twenty years of my life had any of my records; it was like I had never existed before 1974 as far as the National Health was concerned. I did, however, find a report from Dr Esme MacDonald, a psychiatrist who had come to see me in the first flat I ever had on my own in 1977, when I was twenty-three years old.

'I found Thomas looking fairly helpless and hopeless and abjectly miserable,' she wrote at the time. 'He offered little in the way of spontaneous information, and it was with difficulty that I pieced together the details of his history. He eventually told me that he was unable to sleep, he would lie in bed for two or three hours before dozing off and then would waken early. He cried frequently.'

I could remember those times very clearly, because they never stopped. If you are depressed and unable to sleep the days and nights seem to last for ever. It sometimes feels like I have been crying all my life. It was almost as if, from reading her words, I could see that sad young man sitting in front of her.

I took all the material I could to the solicitors to help them prepare my case. Another one of Murphy's victims was already pressing his claim for compensation, but he was demanding a trial by jury, which was slowing the process down because the authorities didn't think a jury would be able to cope with such a complex case. My solicitor, Richard McFarlane, advised me not to go that route and as a result my case came up quicker and I was the first of the St Margaret's boys to have his story heard individually. Most of the others had ended up accepting payments of around £8,000 in return for a promise of silence, but I still wasn't willing to accept that, even if my stubbornness meant that I had to endure living through the whole thing again in front of a judge. I didn't think that £8,000 was a fair recompense for what they had done to us. The council was supposed to have been looking after our best interests when we were little more than babies, but they delivered us up to evil people and many of our lives had been wrecked as a result.

In the final year of my case Anthony Anderson took over representing me as my solicitor from Richard McFarlane when Richard moved onto the bench as a Sheriff. Barrister Robert Hayhow did all the spadework but when he heard that Fife Council had secured the services of a top QC he suggested I should do the same and brought in a man called Andrew Smith as senior advocate.

My case had to be heard in Scotland, since that was where everything had taken place, and I wanted Heather to be by my side all the time. I didn't think I would be able to face all the questions unless she was there with me. But that meant we had to drive up and down from Ashington each day because we didn't have anyone to leave our animals with. At that time we had two dogs and two parrots. The long hours of travelling were adding to the stress, stretching my nerves to breaking point, but I was determined to keep going and not to give up. Because of the long drive we were having to get up early and return home late and I was suffering from a lack of sleep, which increased the sense of confusion and disorientation I felt when I was in the courtroom.

Ever since the memories had returned I had been waking in the night from bad dreams, all sorts of unleashed demons whirling around inside my head, leaving me sweating, panting, crying and anxious in the dark. It was so tempting just to give up the whole struggle but I knew I had to see it through. This was my last chance to get some justice and to make at least some sense of my past life and why it had turned out the way it had.

The courtroom was surprisingly small, with old-fashioned wooden benches, and seemed to be full of people all through the six days that I was giving my evidence, although they somehow managed to keep it from the press. Fife Council were accepting that they had a responsibility to give me compensation for the things Murphy had done to me, all they were arguing about was how much damage he had done to me long-term. Their lawyers were hoping to prove that some of the damage could have been caused at the other places I went to, or that I was the way I was for genetic reasons, meaning I had inherited my problems from Mum and Dad, and that Murphy's treatment of me only made a limited difference. The judge was basically going to decide who had done the most to ruin my childhood, and once that decision had been reached they would assess what my life was worth.

I was worried about how I would come across in court and whether they would believe me. Even though Murphy had been proven guilty, they might still think I was making things up about him for my own benefit, feeling safe because he couldn't argue with me from beyond the grave. Would I be able to explain convincingly to them the damage I thought had been done to me when I could hardly even explain it to myself?

As we went in through the door of the Court of Sessions on the first day, Andrew Smith, who knew everything about my case, including the fact that Murphy had penetrated me, took me to one side.

'This is your last chance to tell the whole truth, Tom,' he said. 'Once this case is over you won't be able to come back in a few years and say you were penetrated if you have denied it under oath in this court. If you don't speak the truth publicly now you never will be able to.'

I knew he was right, but I still didn't know if I was going to be able to do it, particularly when I saw that my case had been allocated to a female judge, Lady Paton. I don't know why it feels so much harder to talk about such things in front of a woman, but for me it does. Even as I was standing in front of her my mind was still racing back and forth. I tried to talk myself into being brave and speaking up, and it felt like I was a child again, trying to force myself to hold my hands out for the strap. I had a horrible feeling that even though I had every intention of speaking honestly, when the moment came to open my mouth the words still might not come out and I would be left feeling like I had been a coward again.

But Lady Paton turned out to be very kind and seemed to understand the way a child's mind would work. She was patient when I was unable to stop myself from crying in the witness box. When I finally had to break down and admit that Murphy had penetrated me I felt just like that small boy screaming

332

into the pillow again. I felt like I was little Tommy, humiliated and hurting and ashamed all over again. Now I had the added shame of having to admit that I had lied about it to the police when they questioned me, which obviously weakened my credibility and I was afraid it might make it look like I was an unreliable witness.

The lawyer working for the council was trying to persuade the judge, and me, that my problems might have stemmed from other institutions I had attended outside the Fife area, particularly my experiences in Oakbank where the boys slipped in and out of one another's beds in search of mutual pleasure. But there was never any physical force involved in the Oakbank seductions, just bribery and persuasion. I couldn't accept that it could have damaged me in any lasting way, particularly as I ended up living my life as a heterosexual.

After a gruelling week in court, putting forward my case and struggling to remain patient with the badgering of the defence counsel, I had no idea whether we were winning or losing the battle.

Fife Council's legal team then asked Lady Paton for

permission to have me examined by an expert witness on their behalf, wanting to challenge what all the doctors and psychologists and psychiatrists had said in my defence. It would mean an agonising delay before I knew the outcome of my case.

Lady Paton granted the request and I was sent to see yet another psychiatrist, a lady who was said to specialise in cases like mine. It took a year to get an appointment with her, so I had plenty of time to check out her past record on the Internet before our meeting. I discovered that she was well known for writing about false memory syndrome, the term for the fiercely contested idea describing a state of mind wherein sufferers have vivid but false memories, often of abusive events during their childhood. Consequently I went into the interview feeling defensive and suspicious of her motives after a long and frustrating year's wait. When she told me, categorically, that 'an adult's penis cannot fit into a child's anus', as if every child who claimed such things was making it up, I could hardly believe my ears. The report she produced confirmed my misgivings. Reading her words actually made me cry and feel physically sick.

'There is no doubt that Wilson was sexually abused by Murphy,' she wrote. 'If the court agrees with my view that the more serious allegation of penetration is not reliable, then the confirmed abuse is largely of fondling, hugging and touching . . . it is perfectly possible that at the time this was not experienced as unpleasant or alarming. It may even have been comforting and have represented the only affection Mr Wilson had ever experienced. There is some support for this view in his later making contact with Murphy from Peterhead. If this were the case it is unlikely that such abuse would have any long-term consequences.'

The idea that I might have taken comfort from the things that Murphy did to me completely knocked the breath out of me. The report ended with the words, 'any physical abuse will have outweighed sexual abuse such as fondling and touching (which may even have been a beneficial influence), and the emotional deprivation will have outweighed both.'

Was it possible that Lady Paton was going to believe this? That she would rule that Murphy hadn't done me any harm at all, that he might actually have been doing me some good?

It took me nearly a month to find the strength to write out for my solicitors some answers to the psychiatrist's suggestions.

Having waited a year to get the appointment and the report, we then had to wait a further five months before my case resumed, leaving us in limbo for nearly a year and a half without knowing what my fate was going to be.

After spending so long in a sort of suspended state, not knowing which way my life was going to go next, whether I was going to be told I was a liar and deserved no compensation, or whether I was going to be told I was right and that the council had done me a serious injury with their decision to put me at Murphy's mercy, Heather and I returned to the courts. This time the press were there and seemed to know all about me.

We were put into a waiting room and left there without any explanation of what the delay was about. The case had been due to resume at ten thirty in the morning and we were sitting waiting to be called, but the time passed and no one came for us. Everyone else seemed to be busy in meetings and rushing around but no one involved us. Eventually Andrew Smith emerged with the news that after reviewing all the evidence Fife Council had started to think differently about their position. They must have decided that the psychiatrist's suggestion that I had enjoyed being abused by Murphy wasn't going to stand up in court and that there was more of a case for them to answer than they had imagined; they couldn't pass the blame for my condition off onto anyone else and they were going to have to take responsibility for messing up my life. Andrew told me they didn't want to go back into court; they wanted to settle, if we could just agree on a figure.

It felt wonderful to know that someone was actually going to accept responsibility for what had happened to me. At last I had an official explanation for why my life had turned out the way it had, why I had spent nearly half my adult years in institutions of one sort or another, apparently unable to mend my ways, constantly struggling against tides of depression. If the council were now willing to accept that their actions had put me in that position, if they weren't even going to try to hide behind the suggestions of their psychiatrist, then they were going to have to accept that they owed me a great deal. I had read of cases where people who had been wrongly convicted of crimes and had served time before the mistake was discovered, had later been awarded hundreds of thousands of pounds in compensation. I felt that little Tommy had been wronged in much the same way. I wasn't willing just to be bought off with a token few thousand.

Andrew Smith went back to talk to them again and emerged to say they had offered to pay me a hundred thousand pounds. Even though it sounded like a lot of money and I was tempted to say yes, just to put an end to the whole painful business, I held my nerve and told him I didn't think that was enough. I didn't want it to seem like I was being greedy, or that I was just in it for what I could get, but I thought the amount should fairly reflect the suffering that I, and many others, had gone through at Murphy's hands. To my relief Andrew didn't seem to disagree and disappeared back into the other room. The next time he came out it was to tell us the council had increased the offer to a hundred and twenty thousand.

'I've given this a lot of thought,' I told him, 'and the least I am willing to accept is a hundred and fifty thousand and they're getting away lightly with that.'

Nodding his understanding, he went back in and returned with the deal agreed. I'm guessing they must have thought they would end up having to pay a lot more if they allowed the case to continue in court.

It sounds like a big settlement, certainly I'd never had money like it before, and it was the largest that any Scottish council had ever paid for a child abuse claim, but when you think that what they did to me marred my whole life and divide the sum by fifty, which was roughly the number of years I had been suffering, it puts it more into proportion. Three thousand pounds for each year of my life does not seem excessive.

I wasn't even that bothered about when the money would come or what I would do with it when it did. It was just such a huge relief that it was all over. It felt like I might finally be able to put the memories to rest in my mind, filed in a healthier place than before. Both Heather and I felt that I had been vindicated and that the long wait had been worth it. There had been so many times when one or other of us had wanted to give up along the way and the other had had to hold steady. The ordeal had put our relationship to the ultimate test and we felt that it had passed.

When the settlement money arrived the solicitors advised us to invest it all in Scottish Widows and save it up for later life, and to start with we took their advice. Heather and I went to Flamingo Land for a break to get our breath back after all we'd been through, and once we were there, back in the place where we'd had so many happy times with the kids, we relaxed and spent some time talking about what we really wanted to do with the next part of our lives together. We decided to invest some of the money in a static caravan and live there virtually all year round, escaping from the council estate in Ashington which had been our home and which seemed to be becoming more and more dangerous and squalid as the drug culture tightened its grip.

Moving to Flamingo Land was like a dream come true; a clean, safe home in a place where most people only get to come on their holidays. Talking to other people who lived and worked on the site, we decided that it would be a good idea to invest the rest of our money in buying a couple more caravans there and renting them out to holidaymakers to give ourselves some regular income.

Our life is peaceful now, living just below the loops of the big dipper. Heather and I don't do any of the rides — we never have gone in for that sort of thing. We just like living in a permanent holiday atmosphere, and walking across the park to the zoo in the evening with our Yorkshire terrier on a lead, watching the lions, giraffes and chimpanzees, and the happy crowds of visitors.

I don't have to retreat into my head so often now, because I don't need to escape from the world I have found.

Epilogue

There are still hundreds of cases of alleged child abuse in children's homes waiting to be heard in Scotland, so many that the courts can't find the time to get to them all. I was lucky that my case was heard when it was. It could easily have been delayed for technical reasons by several years. Murphy himself nearly got away with his sins. Had he managed to delay the trial for a couple more years he would have gone to the grave with his reputation still largely intact. We who had suffered at his hands would all have known what sort of man he really was, but the outside world might well have assumed he was innocent, having not been proved guilty. The locals in St Monans might very well have decided to go ahead with erecting his statue.

It makes you wonder how many other monsters like Murphy manage to go through life being hailed as heroes simply because none of their victims can find the words to speak out, and because everyone else is too busy to take the time to check up on them. I hope that my story may convince other silent victims that they should persevere in their quest for justice, that if they find the courage to tell their stories honestly they will eventually be believed and then they will no longer have to feel ashamed of events in the past for which they were not in any way to blame.

If I Am Missing or Dead

Janine Latus

**A *Sunday Times* and *New York Times* bestselling memoir
– both heartbreaking and inspirational**

In April 2002, Janine Latus's youngest sister, Amy, wrote a note and taped it to the inside of her desk drawer. 'If I am gone or dead', it read, 'question Ron'.

Since childhood Janine and Amy had been sexualised and belittled. As adults the sisters sought familiarity, ending up in a series of abusive relationships. Finally, Janine confessed the truth to Amy, and with her support, escaped in time. But Amy was keeping a terrible secret of her own and by the time the letter was found ten weeks later, she was already missing . . .

'From the first line I was captured and couldn't put the book down. In these pages is the echo of so many other stories I have known . . . You will walk taller from these pages. A story of heartbreak and liberation.'
Julie Gregory, author of *Sickened*

arrow books

Betrayed

Lyndsey Harris with Andrew Crofts

A mother. A daughter. A family torn apart

For the first six years of her life, Sarah Harris was a happy and popular little girl. Until she became the target of a dangerous but invisible enemy – and her life became a living hell. Before long she was suspended from school, alienated from her friends, and terrified of herself.

For her mother, Lyndsey, it was a life beyond her worst nightmares. The daughter she loved so much seemed to have transformed overnight into a child she was almost scared of. Her little girl was doing the unthinkable: stealing razor blades, attempting to poison her friends, even accusing her parents of sexual abuse.

Soon Lyndsey's marriage was on the verge of collapse, social services stepped in, and Lyndsey was fighting to keep her family together – and to save her daughter's sanity. But worse was to come as Lyndsey discovered her family had been victims of the most hurtful betrayal of all . . .

'A really shocking story . . . deeply disturbing' Judy Finnigan

'Beautifully told . . . a good read' Richard Madelay

'Extraordinary . . . an uplifting testament to how a family can survive a nightmare that came so close to breaking them.'
Daily Express

arrow books

Sickened

Julie Gregory

The true story of a lost childhood

A young girl is perched on the cold chrome of yet another doctor's examining table, missing yet another day of school. Just twelve, she's tall, skinny, and weak. Her mother, on the other hand, seems curiously excited. She's about to suggest open heart surgery on her child to 'get to the bottom of this'. She checks her teeth for lipstick and, as the doctor enters, shoots the girl a warning glance. This child will not ruin her plans.

From early childhood, Julie Gregory was continually X-rayed, medicated and operated on in the vain pursuit of an illness that was created in her mother's mind: Munchausen by Proxy, the world's most hidden and dangerous form of child abuse.

'An appalling, fascinating story, expertly told'
Sunday Times

'It blazes with truth and anger . . . a true story of survival and achievement against the odds'
Sunday Telegraph

'Extraordinary . . . shocking and moving'
Woman & Home

'Horrifying but compelling'
Cosmopolitan

'A harrowing but compelling account of the way her mother stole her childhood'
Irish Times

arrow books